Guita  ;

Stop Struggling & Start Learning How to Play the Guitar Faster Than You Ever Thought Possible.

Includes, Songs, Scales, Chords

Tommy Swindali

Discover "How to Find Your Sound"

http://musicprod.ontrapages.com/

Swindali music coaching/Skype lessons.

Email djswindali@gmail.com for info and pricing

Table of Contents

Introduction

Learning to play the guitar is a highly rewarding hobby. Many guitar students who take up the challenge are overwhelmed by the knowledge and commitment that is required to learn to play the guitar successfully. As a result, most guitar students invest in guitar lessons. However, the problem with taking guitar lessons is that it comes with a number of risks. Although most guitar coaches may be experts at playing the guitar, their ability to pass on the knowledge and skills to guitar students can really vary. Therefore, finding a great guitar coach is a very difficult task, with most guitar students ending up being disappointed.

Most beginners turn to self-learning since taking up guitar lessons can be a highly time-consuming, overwhelming, and often a fruitless effort. There is a high chance of ending up with a guitar coach who is a wannabe rock star without having the ability to properly guide guitar students toward mastering the skills of playing the guitar. Many guitar coaches and students don't realize the fact that every good guitarist isn't a good guitar teacher.

Some guitar students try to learn the guitar by solely relying on YouTube videos. While it is true that YouTube videos are often helpful, solely relying on them to learn the guitar can be frustrating due to the sheer amount of videos that are on YouTube with incorrect or inadequate information and advice. Furthermore, most YouTube video tutorials are simply too fast for beginners to grasp the information and guitar students learning to play the guitar using poor techniques and without gaining enough knowledge.

It is highly likely that a guitar student is already frustrated with struggling to play the guitar. They may have tried different options such as guitar coaches, guitar learning websites, and YouTube tutorials without much success. They may have tried very hard to learn the guitar while investing their time and money without reaching their goals and expectations. Such students can benefit from an in-depth, easy-to-understand, and most importantly, fun guide to learning the guitar to help them finally achieve their dream of playing the guitar.

Therefore, guitar students must refer to an in-depth guide that contains everything that they need to know to learn to play the guitar successfully. A good guide to the guitar should help students focus on getting their mindset right and purchasing a good guitar before they get started. They must also be provided with a thorough understanding of music theory, including the anatomy of the guitar and how different frets, strings, and fingers are named and denoted in tablature.

Music theory can be very boring unless they are taught using simple and fun methods. Guitar exercises should also be quick and fun without painful, boring, and repetitive exercises. Learning the guitar should be a fun exercise so that guitar students look forward to training every day without despising it. Making guitar learning fun ensures that guitar students can sustain training long enough to gain the skills that they require to play the guitar well.

It's of utmost importance that a guitar guide a beginner refers to is written and taught by experts. They should be provided with a thorough understanding of music fundamentals and guitar knowledge so that they can start playing notes and chords. The duration that a guitar guide takes from providing fundamental knowledge to getting students to play the guitar needs to be short so that the student does not find the process too slow, boring, and disheartening.

Topics that are discussed in a guitar guide should also be structured in such a way that guitar students are able to learn and apply what they learn in incremental steps. A proper guitar guide should allow guitar students to learn and apply guitar skills step-by-step without providing too much information while encouraging them to apply what they learn with regular practice. Guitar lessons that are properly structured and focused on application make guitar learning a fun and more productive experience while reducing the chances of students becoming disheartened.

A great guitar guide for beginners should have clear diagrams working as visual aids to help students understand what is described. The lessons should be provided in steps with clear instructions on how to apply what students learn by following the guide. A great guide to the guitar should be a good reason for the reader to have a guitar nearby as they read it. It should also provide all the essential chords, scales, and guitar techniques that the student needs to learn to play the guitar well.

A guide to learning the guitar that is aimed toward beginners must be written by guitar experts who have a wealth of experience teaching their craft. Tommy Swindali is a best-selling music producer and publisher, with many of his publications helping thousands of students learn musical instruments. He understood the importance of creating a guitar guide with the knowledge of guitar experts. As a result, numerous guitarists and expert guitar coaches were enlisted to compile this guide.

This guide to playing the guitar for beginners offers them a range of benefits. It begins by providing thorough knowledge about music theory while helping guitar students to understand different types of guitars that exist so that they can purchase the right guitar. It then goes on to clearly describe the anatomy of the guitar and methods to tune a guitar with clear instructions.

This guide provides guitar students a wealth of knowledge when it comes to guitar chords, scales, and techniques. Upon reading, understanding, and applying the information and instructions provided, guitar students will gradually gain the skills that will open up millions of songs they can play on the guitar. Different types of chords, scales, and techniques are well-structured in this guide so that the reader can learn in simple and small incremental steps while ensuring the application of knowledge that they gain. After all, learning to play the guitar is a "hands-on" effort.

Most guitar guides provide good enough information but fail to realize that guitar students can develop bad habits and incorrect techniques as they are more focused on achieving fast results. This guitar guide focuses on providing clear instructions on good guitar habits and correct techniques so that guitar students become technically sound guitarists. Furthermore, the guide focuses more on providing clear and simple information and instructions with an emphasis on application and training instead of results. The thinking is that consistent application will bring forth the results that students aim to achieve.

The problem with most guitar guides is that students often don't find them enjoyable to read and apply. This guitar guide provides guitar students different songs belonging to various genres so that they can enjoy applying what they learn while increasing their confidence and gaining motivation as they are able to play popular songs that are fun to play and listen to.

There is no better way to achieve perfection than practice. Many guitar students are fixated on purchasing a good guitar and accessories, finding a great guitar coach, guitar guides, and other resources that they forget the most important ingredient of guitar learning, which is practice. How a guitar student practices and how often he or she practices will eventually decide how soon they are going to learn to play the guitar. Therefore, it's very important that guitar students commit to spending at least a few hours every day throughout the course of this book and beyond so that they can master the art of playing the guitar.

Different guitar students aspire to become great guitarists for different reasons. Some may be simply inspired by their favorite artists and bands, while some may want to experience the satisfaction of creating music. Some students may be inspired by social benefits. After all, a man or woman with a guitar is often the life of the party. Good guitarists are loved and valued by their families, friends, and colleagues because their ability to create music makes their presence fun, amusing, and sometimes very welcome.

Some guitar students set out to become a rock star. It's important to remember that almost every rock star guitarist out there started just like you are doing. However, it is unlikely that most such rock stars had a wealth of resources that are available to guitar students today. Therefore, it's safe to say that with proper guidance, a guitar student today has a better shot at becoming a great guitarist or a rock star than a guitar student decades ago.

The reasons and motivating factors behind wanting to play the guitar do not matter. What is important is to recognize those motivating factors and make a promise to give it the best shot. If a guitar student is able to maintain their commitment long enough, they are highly likely to learn the guitar soon enough.

There is no better time to pick up the guitar and play (or practice) than right now! It's time to take action. Make sure that you follow this guide with regular practice sessions. As a matter of fact, it is recommended that you read through this guide with your guitar next to you so that you can apply what you learn simultaneously.

So what are you waiting for? Get your guitar and start practicing and playing. You may not sound good in the beginning. You may face a few bumps along the way. Watch out for plateaus because there will be a few. It may seem like you are not making much progress until you suddenly realize that your fingers are responding faster. The difference between smoothly changing chords can be a day or a week. Therefore, giving up should not be an option.

So read this book while regularly applying what you learn along the way. Read important chapters a few times because what's more important is to learn things correctly rather than how fast you learn or how fast you can play. Get to work and embark on the journey to becoming the rock star you always dreamed of becoming!

Chapter 1: Getting Started

The ability to play a musical instrument is one of the most rewarding and self-satisfying skills that any individual can invest in. Almost every human being enjoys music. Being able to play an instrument gives people the ability to recreate the music they like by themselves. It is one of the most satisfying activities known to humankind.

The guitar is one of the most popular musical instruments on the planet. The music guitars make is highly appealing. It is also an instrument that is very popular thanks to its widespread use in most forms and genres of music. As a result, most individuals who are keen to learn to play a musical instrument turn to the guitar.

Learning to play the guitar can be a daunting task for a beginner, especially if that person does not have much theoretical knowledge of music. However, even individuals with no background and experience in music can successfully learn to play the guitar. While success awaits at the end of the road, it is certainly going to be a challenging journey.

Therefore, it is important to approach learning to play the guitar with the right mindset. It's important to understand that it takes time and practice to learn any musical instrument. Playing the guitar requires specific skills that involve the training of the mind, fingers, and even the entire body.

What's So Great About Learning to Play the Guitar?

Various factors encourage people to learn to play the guitar. These may be personal, social, or educational. One of the most common reasons that attract people toward the guitar is its social impact. The guitar has the unique ability to unite people and provide entertainment with an alluring touch of spontaneity. As a result, a person who knows how to play the guitar is often valued by their family, friends, and colleagues. Therefore, an individual may be inspired to learn to play the guitar due to its social benefits.

The guitar is a musical instrument that is widely used in popular music. It is safe to say that the majority of popular genres of music involve the guitar in one way or another. Therefore, individuals who enjoy popular music may be inspired by their favorite artists, bands, and musicians.

Being able to play the guitar brings so many personal benefits. A man or woman who knows how to play the guitar will hardly be bored. All they need to do is to pick up their guitar and play it. Learning to play the guitar and advancing toward more difficult techniques and playing difficult songs can be very self-satisfying.

Learning to play the guitar is a difficult task. Therefore, starting as a beginner and moving to the intermediate level can be considered as a great personal achievement. The skill of playing the guitar is a skill that sticks for life. It is similar to learning a language. Upon reaching the intermediate level, it is very difficult or, in most cases, almost impossible to forget how to learn the guitar, although regular training is always advised. An intermediate player is likely to lose touch but rarely lose their skill.

When a guitarist is playing, their mind is largely focused on the music they are creating and the movements of their fingers, hands, and feet. Therefore, playing the guitar is a hobby that offers many mental health benefits. Playing the guitar is highly recommended for those who are dealing with anxiety, stress, and depression as it helps them become more relaxed and provides them with a soothing escape.

Those who are starting to learn the guitar may be required to follow specific instructions at first. However, as they progress and reach the intermediate level, an entire world of creativity and experimentation opens up for them. As a result, intermediate guitar players often benefit from improvisation and creativity by playing the guitar.

Playing the guitar can be physically demanding. Perhaps not as much as playing a sport, but it does involve more pain than most people ever imagine. Beginners are likely to experience pain in their fingers, palms, and hands, although they will wear off as they improve. Playing the guitar requires the fingers, hands, and even feet to be in sync with the brain. As a result, playing the guitar is an activity that offers a lot more physical health benefits than it may at first appear.

Learning the guitar requires consistent training. It forces individuals to be more organized with their time. As a result, learning to play the guitar indirectly results in people being more organized and professional. They are highly likely to attend to their duties so that they have the time to play the guitar for an hour or so every day.

Make the Commitment

The first step to start learning the guitar is to make the commitment. It is going to take time. The fingers and hands are going to hurt, and there will be many obstacles to overcome, not to mention the research and experimentation involved. There will be many days where clear improvements may not be seen or heard. However, the trick is to be patient and keep at it.

Those are the most important ingredients of learning to play the guitar; patience and persistence.

It's important to have a good guitar to learn how to play it. Once the commitment is made towards learning the guitar, the best option is to go ahead and purchase a guitar instead of borrowing one. It will confirm the commitment made toward learning the guitar and act as a motivating factor to keep going, especially when things don't seem to be improving at all. No one likes to own a guitar and not know how to play it. Therefore, they are more likely to give it their best shot before they give up on it.

Guitars come in all sizes and shapes. They can also be bought for different price ranges. Beginners must purchase a guitar that isn't cheap but also not super expensive. Visiting the guitar store and going for a moderately priced guitar is the best option.

Cheap guitars may not require a huge initial investment. However, they may not sound great, or they might make it difficult for a beginner to learn to play the guitar. As a result, it is recommended that beginners invest in a good guitar without breaking the bank. Most guitar shops offer packages for beginners that include good guitars and essential accessories that they might need.

There are plenty of resources to utilize when learning to play the guitar. A wealth of online resources await you once you start learning. It's also easy to find guitar coaches and classes in any city. Furthermore, most people are likely to have a friend or two who know how to play the guitar. It is highly recommended to ask such a friend to tag along when visiting musical instrument shops for the purpose of buying a guitar so that they can provide the required guidance.

Common Challenges When Learning to Play the Guitar

New guitar players are often faced with a number of challenges that are both physical, psychological, and sometimes social. While it's important to be patient and persistent throughout the beginner stage, it's important to have an understanding of the challenges that await you down the road so that you can face and overcome those obstacles successfully.

The Urge to Give Up

It is impossible to learn to play the guitar in a few days. Some naturally talented and musically gifted individuals may indeed learn to play the guitar faster than others. However, there isn't an average time frame for someone to learn the guitar. The progress is usually determined by a number of factors such as the time invested for training and learning, the quality of learning and application, prior experience with musical instruments, music knowledge, the physical strength of hands and fingers, the mental strength to focus and learn, the environment, and the quality of the guitar and accessories that are used.

If there is anything certain, it is the fact that anyone who learns to play the guitar will think about giving up at some point. Therefore, it's important to remember that there will be bad days or even weeks, where no progress will be evident. However, the trick is to fight through such plateaus without constantly searching for quick progress.

The Lack of Natural Talent

Many guitar students are inspired by naturally gifted and talented musicians. Some such guitarists were indeed born with the gift of music and guitar playing skills. However, not every successful guitarist is naturally gifted. There many famous guitarists who have made up for the lack of natural talent with hard work. Therefore, guitar students need to understand that natural talent isn't a must to learn to play guitar.

Some beginner guitarists may find it difficult to identify notes and chords or when to play them. Some may find it difficult to strum to a rhythm, and some may have difficulties with identifying pitches. However, with practice, they are highly likely to improve. Therefore, even if a guitar student isn't naturally gifted, they can still go on to learn the guitar successfully.

The Lack of Practice and Focus

One of the main causes of failure when learning to play the guitar is due to the lack of practice and focus. Guitar students first need to allocate some time every day to progress their skills. Consistent practice is very important, especially during the beginner stages. Furthermore, it's important to keep guitar practice sessions to comfortable lengths as long sessions can become unproductive due to fatigue and reduced focus.

Therefore, guitar students are highly recommended to allocate some time for training every day. It can be a one-hour session or two 30-minute sessions. The objective is to maintain focus throughout each session so that they can improve their skills incrementally every day.

Failing or Trying Too Hard to Build Finger Callus

Calluses on the fingertips of guitarists take time to develop. They are important features of a guitarist as they protect the fingertips from hurting while pressing down notes and are a natural part of the learning process. Beginners will start their guitar learning journey without finger calluses. Therefore, it's important to pace their training slowly for the first two to three weeks until they develop finger calluses.

There are numerous myths regarding speeding up the development of finger calluses. Many beginners practice such methods and end up hurting their fingers, and that hampers their guitar training. Therefore, it's important to be patient until finger calluses are naturally developed without trying to speed up the natural process. Once developed, finger calluses can last for weeks or even months without playing the guitar. However, regular practice is highly prescribed to maintain finger calluses so that guitarists can play the guitar comfortably.

Impatience

Guitar students need to understand that the initial stages of learning to play the guitar will sometimes take much longer than they expect. Some students will find it difficult to move their fingers, and that makes changing chords very difficult. Therefore, it will take a long time, sometimes months, until they can properly play a song.

The trick is to be patient and stick to playing simple chords while switching between them. Students will indeed be itching to start playing songs. However, it is better to make sure that they can transition between chords quickly before doing so to avoid disappointment.

The process of changing chords requires muscle memory. A guitar student will not have muscle memory when they start playing the guitar. The trick is to make sure that they play each chord correctly while slowly changing chords. With practice, the time between chord transitions will slowly decrease. Soon enough, they will be able to smoothly and quickly change chords and move on to playing songs.

Wrong Technique

Being a technically correct guitarist from the beginner stage enables guitar students to progress in their guitar training quickly and comfortably. Therefore, it's important to pay close attention to learning about the correct techniques related to holding the guitar, posture, holding notes and chords, holding the pick, and correct strumming. When a guitar student becomes technically correct in the beginning, they will not only progress faster and easier but also avoid painful and time-consuming changes to their techniques down the road.

Poor Application

Guitar learning is all about learning notes and chords so that they can be applied to create music. However, some guitar students try to learn too much without applying what they learn. Some beginners try to learn dozens of chords before they progress to actually playing a song. What they don't realize is the fact that dozens of songs can be easily played with three or four chords.

Therefore, it's important to plan their learning so that they can learn a few chords, practice changing between those chords, apply them by playing a song, and finally proceed to learn a new chord or two. The process can be repeated where they apply the chords by playing new songs. The application makes the process of learning to play the guitar more enjoyable, satisfactory, and motivational. The lack of application takes the fun out of it, and that usually results in beginners giving up.

Being Limited to Certain Genres

Guitar students need to be open to playing songs that they may not love when starting to play the guitar. Some students may be into genres such as punk rock and death metal. If they limit themselves during the beginner stages to playing songs from such genres, their progress may be slow since there may not be that many song choices suitable for beginners. Furthermore, favoring one or a handful of genres may limit the skills that guitar students need to learn.

For example, a guitar student who only likes listening to punk rock will find it difficult to play most punk rock songs with open chords. As a result, they may learn power chords without properly learning open chords. Doing so will not only make their guitar learning incomplete but also avoid them gaining valuable skills that are essential for a guitarist.

Therefore, guitar students need to be open to listening to and playing songs belonging to genres that they may not like. It makes their guitar learning more complete. Once they master different chords and get closer to the intermediate level, they can focus on one or a few genres. However, until then, they need to be more open to different genres, such as country, classical, pop, blues, jazz, funk, progressive, punk rock, soft rock, etc.

Social Barriers

Various social factors can get in the way of guitar training. Some guitar students may not be able to practice properly due to their surroundings. A beginner does not sound great when learning to play the guitar. Therefore, the sound of them practicing the guitar may not be pleasant for his or her family members and neighbors. Guitar students must find a quiet place and times during the day that help them to practice without being interrupted while also ensuring that the people around them are also not affected.

The Lack of Confidence

Most guitar students lack confidence that results in their unwillingness to showcase their guitar playing skills to others. A beginner may only know how to play one or two songs. However, they need to remember that whatever the skills are that they may have gained, these are valuable no matter what. Therefore, it's important for guitar students to be proud of what they learn and confidently showcase their skills when the moment arises. If they face ridicule and criticism, they can positively ignore such negativity given the fact that they are still learning to play the guitar.

Learning Strategy

This guide to guitar-learning for beginners aims to take guitar students through a complete journey where they gain the knowledge, advice, and tips required to successfully learn to play the guitar and progress to the intermediate level. The first chapter was intended toward preparing guitar students for the memorable, enjoyable, and challenging journey ahead.

The guitar is a musical instrument. Therefore, a good understanding of music theory is essential to learn successfully and sustainably to play the guitar. The second chapter intends to provide the reader with a thorough knowledge of melodies, chords, rhythms, scales, majors and minors, and more. It's highly recommended that students pay close attention to music theory and have a good understanding before they proceed to the next chapter.

Most guitar students are likely to start learning with an acoustic guitar. However, it's important to remember that guitars come in all sizes and shapes while producing different sounds. Chapter three intends to educate the reader regarding different types of guitars categorized as acoustic guitars and electric guitars. Furthermore, the chapter discusses different parts of a guitar, especially names and numbers that are used to indicate different guitar strings and fingers.

Most guitar students often find themselves being clueless regarding the type of guitar they are going to purchase. Buying the first guitar must be done with careful consideration. Chapter three provides useful and important steps that guitar students need to keep in mind when purchasing their first guitar.

A guitar needs to be tuned correctly for it to create notes in the correct pitches and for chords to sound correct. However, most beginners often find it difficult to not only tune their guitars but also identify if a guitar is properly tuned or not. Chapter four provides simple tips to identify if a guitar is in tune or not and tune it using a variety of methods.

Open chords are some of the easiest chords to play on the guitar. Chapters five and six explains Major Open Chords and Minor Open Chords, respectively. Analysis, terminology, history, and famous uses, techniques, and fingering are explained so that the reader gains a thorough knowledge about open chords and finds learning to play open chords easier.

Power chords are a type of chords that are often used in popular music. Chapter six is dedicated to educating the reader regarding power chords, their terminology, history, and famous uses, techniques, and fingering. Upon completing chapter six, the reader should have a thorough understanding of power chords and use the tips provided to start playing them successfully.

Barre chords are considered to be the bridge that takes beginner guitar students to the intermediate level. Many guitar students find barre chords challenging as they not only involve all four fingers of the left hand but also put significant strain on the fingers and palm. Poor technique can also contribute to the difficulties experienced when playing barre chords.

Chapter eight discusses what barre chords are, their terminology, and history and famous uses to give the reader a good understanding of what barre chords are, where they originated, and their evolution in music. The chapter also discusses techniques and fingering in simple terms to enable the reader to play barre chords successfully.

Other Chords

Most guitar students are so focused on the left hand, which is used to hold notes and chords that they often pay little attention to the right hand that is used for strumming. Chapter 10 provides the reader with a good understanding of the correct techniques for the strumming hand and tips on how to strum correctly, including basic strumming, chord changing, finger strumming, and more.

Guitar pick is a tool that is used to assist strumming while creating a bright sound compared to the sound that fingertip strumming and plucking creates. Chapter 11 takes the reader through the basics of a guitar pick or plectrum, including the correct techniques to hold the pick and different types of picks out there. Chapter 11 also discusses the correct techniques and posture for the left hand. You will also find the following information in the next four chapters:

- Chapter 12: Single-Notes Patterns

- Chapter 13: Open Position Scales

- Chapter 14: Articulations

- Chapter 15: Improvisation

Guitar students can benefit from opening their minds to different genres of music. It not only makes their musical tastes more diverse but also makes them more complete guitarists. Chapter 16 takes the reader through different genres, including Blues, Rock, Country, Punk, Classical, Jazz, and World Scales.

Most beginners find it difficult to select songs that are ideal for their level. Some guitar students try to play difficult songs and become discouraged. Chapter 17 takes the reader through a number of songs belonging to different genres that the reader can play, starting from the very beginning until they reach the intermediate level.

Learning to play the guitar is a journey that is filled with many challenges. It also requires guitar students to be focused, organized, motivated, disciplined, and curious along the way. However, most importantly, guitar learning needs to be fun. This learning strategy aims to not only provide guitar students with the education they require to learn to play the guitar but also offers a lot of fun along the way.

Chapter 2: Music Theory - Made Fun!

Let's face it; music theory can be boring for many, especially guitar students who don't have a background in music. As a result, most guitar students tend to skip music theory lessons or simply skim through and proceed to "more interesting" guitar lessons. However, it's important to face the fact that music theory plays a vital role in a guitar student's success in learning to play the guitar.

Furthermore, theoretical knowledge in music will ultimately determine how far a guitar student will go. Therefore, any guitar student who is hoping to play the guitar well, play different songs, especially difficult ones, and get close to being an advanced guitarist needs to have a good understanding of music theory.

Music theory is also a very broad subject. As a result, comprehensively learning music theory can take a very long time. Therefore, it's important that beginners only learn what is essential for them to learn to play the guitar and reach the intermediate level. Any other more advanced music theory lessons can be learned down the road as the need arises.

Furthermore, some music theory lessons are more related to certain genres, such as classical, jazz, and world music. Guitar students are advised to be open about the genres that they play and practice during their learning stages. As such, specific music theory lessons can be left to be learned later when those students become more advanced, allowing them to focus on such genres.

The easiest way to make music theory fun is by only exploring music theory that is essential to learning the guitar and reaching the intermediate level. Doing so reduces the amount that a guitar student needs to learn to result in the lessons being short and sweet. Furthermore, music theory should be revisited every few months until a student can clearly remember and apply it to their playing.

The basis of music theory is made up of physics related to sound. Music is the art of creating sounds. Therefore, understanding the simple physics of sound can make learning music theory much easier.

Guitar students who do not have any or who have very little background in music will need to pay close attention to this chapter. Some students may have learned music a long time ago. Therefore, thoroughly reading this chapter is important to such students to refresh their memory. However, they are highly likely to remind themselves of their past lessons quickly. It's important to highlight that all guitar students read this chapter carefully irrespective of their knowledge and background in music theory.

Think of music theory as being similar to what grammar is to a language. A grammatically correct person sounds clear and is able to communicate well. Their use of language is fluid, smooth, and effortless. Similarly, a guitarist who has a clear and correct understanding of music theory will be able to create music that is of high quality. Furthermore, they will find understanding and feeling music much easier.

Pitch

The relative degree of how high or low a sound is known as its pitch. Theoretically, it is the rate of vibrations that a sound creates. Pitch is closely related to how accurate a particular note is. A particular note played on the guitar represents a specific scientific pitch that can be measured in Hertz.

For example, play the note "A" on the open fourth string. Then play the note "A" on the second fret by holding down the G string (3rd string) on the second fret. Comparing these two sounds will showcase how the sound created by playing the open string A note is lower than the sound created by playing the same note on the second fret.

When a guitar is out of tune, the notes that are played differ from their correct or natural pitch. As a result, a guitar can be tuned by listening to a correct note and comparing the sound of the same note with the sounds that the guitar creates. When both the sounds have the same pitch, the guitar is in tune.

Rhythm

The way sounds are organized in relation to time is known as the rhythm. Therefore, any proper organization of sounds consists of a rhythm. It can be a song that contains pitches such as the strumming of a guitar to the sounds consistently created by two sticks. Musicians use a beat to play to a rhythm, which is called a tempo. Tempo describes the number of beats per minute. A guitarist playing to a certain tempo only plays a rhythm that fits into that tempo.

For example, a guitarist may strum once per beat or once per two beats according to the tempo they are playing to. In music, beats are divided into equal parts so that musicians understand the sounds that need to be played according to the progression of beats.

Melody

A series of pitches higher than the rest of the sounds or music is known as a melody. Think of a melody as the plot of a drama. It is the main storyline. All musical sounds in a song are do not belong to the melody. Think of it as the characters of a drama and their relationships to the story or plot. Similarly, sounds that do not belong to the melody coexist with it and are important to it. They complement the melody but do not affect it.

The melody is usually the part that a singer sings in a song. It is the factor in music that makes a song memorable. It is easy to forget the lyrics and chords of a song. However, forgetting the melody of a good song is very difficult and rare. The melody is important to guitarists since they usually play to the melody of the song. Chords are arranged in such a way that the melody is played out while the singer sings. Therefore, understanding what a melody is made up of is important for any guitar student.

Harmony

A collection of pitches that ring together creates harmony. Such combinations of pitches contribute to creating sounds that have various moods. Take the example of major versus minor chords. In terms of sound, they may sound very similar. However, the moods they create are entirely different.

A harmony that contains more notes is considered a more complex one. Imagine three guitar players playing different notes. One plays the note C. Another plays the note E while the third guitarist plays the note G. In harmony, they create a C major chord.

Timbre

The quality that gives a sense of uniqueness and distinction to a note is known as Timbre, pronounced as TAM-ber. A guitarist may play the note C. Then a singer will sing a note C. Although both the sounds created were note C, one can easily distinguish between the sound that was played on the guitar and the one that was sung. This is due to Timbre that gives every musical sound a unique character.

Dynamics

The softness or loudness of music is described by Dynamics. A song may include a part that may sound as soft as a whisper followed by a loud chord. Dynamics add character to the music. Although variation in volume isn't often used in today's music, dynamics still play a major role in music when it comes to how it appeals to the listeners and the emotions it induces in them.

Scales

A set of tones that can be used to build melodies and harmonies are known as a Scale in music. The word scale is derived from the Latin word that translates to "Ladder." Scales can create different tonal flavors and moods. There are many different scales in music.

In music theory, a scale organizes a number of notes fundamentally using their pitch and frequency. An ascending scale organizes notes in such a way that the pitch of the notes increases. A descending scale organizes notes the opposite way. A melody or harmony is usually created using the notes belonging to the same scale.

A scale consists of seven notes in traditional Western music. Whole and half-step intervals usually separate the notes in a scale. The more stable and central note of a scale is known as the "tonic" of that scale. The notes of a particular scale can be denoted using the numbers in relation to the number of steps they are away from the tonic.

The C major scale consists of the notes C, D, E, F, G, A, and B. C is the tonic of the scale. The notes of the scale can be labeled as 1, 2, 3, 4, 5, 6, and 7 due to their positions in the scale in relation to the tonic, which is C.

Chapter 3: Types of Guitars

Guitars come in all sizes and shapes. The material that is used to make them also varies. Furthermore, different types of guitars create sound using different mechanisms. Guitars can be easily categorized into two groups as acoustic guitars and electric guitars. Acoustic guitars are hollow and create sounds using the air in their hollow body. Electric guitars, on the other hand, feature hollow or solid bodies but use electricity to amplify their sound.

Guitars have largely evolved over the centuries. Different types of guitars create sound with varying levels of richness and timbres. Some types of guitars are more suited to certain genres as a result. A guitar student may be attracted to a certain type of guitar as a result of their taste in music. For example, a person who loves classical or country music is likely to find acoustic guitars attractive while a person who prefers rock or punk rock may be attracted to electric guitars.

Acoustic Guitars

An acoustic guitar creates sound using its body and strings. Therefore, the sound that is created by acoustic guitars is unique from one guitar to another. Woods such as Mahogany and Rosewood and substitutes such as high-pressure laminate (HPL) are used to make guitars today. The tones that an acoustic guitar creates usually mature with age. However, acoustic guitars made using HPL does mature tonally as much as wooden ones.

It's important to have an idea about the tone that a guitar student prefers when purchasing an acoustic guitar since different acoustic guitars create slightly different tones. While it's advised for beginners to seek the help of a friend who plays the guitar or shop assistants who are knowledgeable, it's important that the student who is purchasing likes the sound a guitar creates.

Acoustic guitars are the most versatile types of guitars since they do not rely on external factors to create sound, such as electric guitars. They can be easily transported and played whenever required. The sound they create is also perfect for those learning to play the guitar.

Acoustic-Electric Guitar

An acoustic-electric guitar is actually an acoustic guitar that provides the option of plugging into an amplifier if required. Modern acoustic-electric guitars are equipped with systems that can help guitarists create more authentic-sounding acoustic tones using the amplifier. It is also common for acoustic-electric guitars to feature EQ controls and tuners. The body of most acoustic-electric guitars features a cutaway to provide easy access to the upper frets of the guitar.

Nylon-String Classical Guitar

Also known as Classical Guitars or Spanish Guitars, these acoustic guitars feature nylon strings. These guitars are ideal for beginners, especially children, since nylon strings create less tension making it easier on the fingertips as most guitar students struggle with steel strings until they develop finger callouses. Nylon-string classical guitars create a soothing and unique tone.

Resonator

These acoustic guitars are highly unique when it comes to their appearance, as well as the mechanism that is used to amplify sound. The vibrations of a resonator's strings are directed into one of three metal cones that result in the amplification of the sound that is created by the guitar. Resonators have wooden or metal bodies, round or square necks, and a single large cone or three smaller ones. Square-neck Resonators are played with the guitarist holding it face up on their lap or any other horizontal surface. Round-neck Resonators are held just like a conventional guitar.

Electric Guitars

Most guitarists would agree that the world of music could have been much less cool if it wasn't for electric guitars. Electric guitars changed the way musicians and the general public thought about guitars. They not only offered a unique and more attractive sound that inspired a range of new genres but also gave guitarists a world of technique and options that were unheard of before.

Hollow Body Guitars

All guitars were acoustic before the 1930s when the electrical amplification of guitars was introduced by Gibson guitars. Charlie Christian is considered the pioneer who introduced the use of amplification as well as the guitar solo. By the 1950s, guitars with pickups were common among jazz guitarists. The 1960s saw the birth of Thin-line Hollow body guitars that were made iconic by John Lennon of Beatles.

Semi-Acoustic or Semi-Hollow

One of the main setbacks of a Hollow body guitar is that they create electronic feedback. Unwanted feedback isn't considered ideal, although deliberate feedback sounds great. It soon became common for Hollow body guitarists to stuff their guitars with various materials such as cotton, wool, newspaper, and even packing peanuts to silence the unwanted feedback.

Ted McCarty of Gibson introduced a better solution in 1958 with the release of the ES-335 model, where a block was designed to run through the body giving birth to semi-hollow guitars. Semi-acoustic or semi-hollow guitars solved the unwanted feedback issue of Hollow body guitars to a great extent. Modern-day semi-hollow guitars are influenced by McCarty's solution.

Solid-Body

The solid-body guitar was one of the most influential and pivoting innovations in the history of guitars. They are tougher, easier to transport and play compared to Hollow body guitars. They also allow guitarists to tailor sounds using different effects. Solid-body electric guitars also look cooler compared to other types of guitars.

Different types of solid-body guitars exist. Therefore, it's important to try them out before purchasing one by carefully considering important factors such as the type of neck (thin, fat, or medium) and their sound. Solid-body guitars also vary in the length of their necks that result in varying string tensions.

The Anatomy of a Guitar

Guitar students must have a good understanding of the different parts of a guitar. The anatomy of guitars has some differences between acoustic and electric guitars since acoustic guitars do not feature amplification. Electric guitars, on the other hand, feature amplification, and as a result, they have unique parts that do not feature on acoustic guitars.

Body

The main part of a guitar that includes the bridge is known as the body of that guitar. In electric guitars, the body includes volume and tone knobs. The easiest way to remember what part the guitar body is to associate it as the part in contact with your body.

Neck

The arm of the guitar that pokes out of its body is known as its neck. Strings run along the neck while frets are located along the surface of the neck. The neck is one of the most fragile parts of a guitar. Therefore, it's important to treat the neck with special care.

Fingerboard

The flatter side of the neck where fingers are placed by guitarists to hold notes and chords is known as the fingerboard. Frets are located along the fingerboard of a guitar. As a result, it is also known as the fretboard.

Headstock

The headstock is located at the end of the guitar's necks. Tuners are usually located on the headstock, which is used to tighten and loosen strings while tuning.

Tuners (Machine Heads)

The knobs that can be turned to loosen or tighten the strings and change their pitch are known as tuners or machine heads. Most guitars feature tuners on the headstock.

Nut

A strip made out of bone, plastic, or metal that separates the fingerboard from the headstock is known as the nut. The area of the strings that can be held down to play notes and chords begin from the nut. In other words, the first fret begins from the nut.

Bridge

The opposite end of the nut is known as the bridge. It is usually made out of metal and lies on the body of the guitar. The balls that connect one end of the strings to the guitar sits on the bridge.

Frets

A fret is a space between two fret wires. Fret wires are the metal strips that divide the fingerboard into different frets. Sometimes, the word "fret" is used to refer to fret wires as well, although such use is technically incorrect.

Position Markers

These markers enable guitarists to quickly identify important locations on the fretboard such as the 3rd, 5th, 7th, and 9th frets. Dots are usually used for position markers, although some guitars feature different symbols for the same purpose. The 12th fret is marked with two dots.

Strap Pin

A button that the guitar strap fits to is known as the strap pin. Strap pins aren't always secure, and therefore, it is advised that a strap lock is used to secure the strap to the pin so that it won't come off, causing the guitar to fall.

Parts of an Acoustic Guitar

The parts described below are only seen on acoustic guitars.

Sound Hole

The opening where the sound comes out of an acoustic guitar is known as the soundhole. The sound that is first generated by the strings is reached into the hollow of the guitar and bounces back out through the soundhole. It's important to ensure that the soundhole isn't obstructed during strumming.

Rose

Most acoustic guitars feature decorations around the soundhole. Some acoustic guitars do not feature a rose.

String Peg

A peg that is usually made of plastic or metal used to hold the strings to the bridge is known as a string peg. Each string has a separate string peg. String pegs must be pressed firmly into the bridge since if they spring out, it can be dangerous for the guitarist.

Scratch Plate (Pick Guard)

A plate usually made using plastic or a similar material protects the body of the guitar from scratches that the fingernails or pick can inflict on the body of the guitar.

Bridge

The bridge of an acoustic guitar is made using wood. It is also bigger than the bridge of an electric guitar.

Saddle

The object provides a resting place for strings on the bridge. Saddles are usually made using bone or plastic.

Cutaway

The lower area of the body located close to the fingerboard is known as the cutaway. The design of the cutaway allows the guitarist to reach upper frets. However, beginners are unlikely to use frets that are that far up the fretboard.

Parts of an Electric Guitar

The parts described below are only seen on electric guitars.

Pick-up(s)

This device picks up the sound that is generated by an electric guitar. It is usually located under an electric guitar's strings. A pick-up contains magnets that allow it to identify the variations in the magnetic fields of the moving strings. Pick-ups come in two types that are single coil and humbucker. Humbuckers usually feature on Gibson guitars and create a fuller sound and less hum. Single coil pick-ups usually feature on Fender guitars.

Pickup Selector

Most electric guitars are equipped with multiple pick-ups. The pickup selector is the device that allows the guitarist to select, which pick-up is being used. It is possible to choose more than one pick-up at a time.

Output Jack Socket

Electric guitars are used with amplifiers. The output jack socket allows the guitarist to plug it into an amplifier. If the cable isn't properly pushed into the socket, it results in a loud static noise.

Volume Knob(s)

The volume of the sound that is generated by the guitar is controlled using volume knobs. If a guitar has multiple pick-ups, it is likely to feature multiple volume knobs.

Tone Knob(s)

These knobs allow the guitarist to control the amount of treble and bass that is created by the guitar. Most guitars feature one or two-tone knobs.

Scratchplate (Pick-plate or Pickguard)

While the scratchplate on an acoustic guitar protects it from scratches caused by the fingernails and pick, the scratchplate on an electric guitar holds all the electronics in place.

'Whammy' Bar

This part is a metal bar that is connected to the bridge of an electric guitar. It allows the guitarist to lower the pitch of notes that are being played by pushing it down. The Whammy bar is one of the most fun and expressive tools on an electric guitar, although its use can be complicated to beginners.

String Tree

The string tree is only seen on some guitars. Strings run under the string tree so that they don't jump off the nut.

Floating Tremolo

A bridge system that is designed to clamp down and lock strings so that they don't go out of tune. However, floating tremolos aren't recommended for beginners. It is usually favored by expert guitarists who perform Whammy bar tricks.

String, Fret, and Finger Numbers

Learning how to read guitar tablature is an important lesson for any guitar student as they will need to refer to diagrams that denote strings, frets, and fingers using numbers. Understanding, which strings, frets, and fingers are represented by specific numbers enables guitar students to play notes, chords, and songs using guitar tablature that is freely available on the Internet.

String Names and Numbers

A student who is learning to play the guitar needs to learn many new concepts, terms, and nomenclature to understand the basics of music and guitar playing. The assigning of numbers or names for different strings makes it easier for guitar students and guitarists to understand which strings they need to hold down and keep open when playing notes and chords.

Most guitars have six strings, especially the ones that are recommended for beginners. The six strings of the guitar are named after the notes they create when played while they are open with the guitar in tune. Their names from the thinnest or the highest-pitched are E, B, G, D, A, and E. Referring to strings using names can sometimes be confusing for beginners since there are two E strings. The thinner string, located at the bottom of the fingerboard when looking down, is the high E, also known as the E 1st. The other E string is the thicker one that is located nearest to the guitarist's eyes when looking down at the fingerboard. It is known as the E 6th. The E 1st creates a higher-pitched note E while the E 6th string creates a lower-pitched note E when played openly.

Referring to guitar strings, numerically, is clearer. The high E string, located at the bottom of the fingerboard is known as the first. Similarly, B string is the 2nd, the G string is the 3rd, the D string is the 4th, the A string is the 5th, and the low E string or the one that is the closest to the guitarist is the 6th.

Fret Numbers

Holding down different strings on different frets create different notes. A combination of such notes creates a chord. Therefore, understanding the numbers of frets is important when learning to play notes and chords. Fret numbers start from the fret that is at the outer edge of the guitar neck or the one that is the closest to the guitar's headstock. The area of the 1st fret is separated by the guitar's "nut" and the first fret wire.

The frets are assigned numbers in ascending order as they move towards the guitar body, such as 2nd, 3rd, 4th, and so on. Fret markers are markings on the fingerboard that enables guitarists to identify different areas of the fingerboard quickly. Fret markers are usually marked at the 3rd, 5th, 7th, 9th, and 12th frets.

When a student understands the numbers that are assigned to each string and fret, they can easily play notes and chords without having to know the name of notes. For example, a guitar student may be asked to play note C that they may not how to play. However, the same instruction can be given as to play the 3rd string on the 3rd fret that results in the guitars student playing the note C.

Finger Numbers

Some chords can indeed be played by using different fingers to hold down different notes. However, most chords can be played in a more organized and comfortable manner by correctly using different fingers to hold down different strings. As a result, fingers are numbered in guitar tablature to ensure that the guitarists, especially beginners, know exactly which finger they should use to hold down a specific note.

Number 1 is assigned for the forefinger, number 2 for the middle finger, number 3 for the ring finger, and number 4 for the pinky. Therefore, when a guitar student wants to play the C chord, they must hold down the 5th string on the 3rd fret with their 3rd finger, 4th string on the 2nd fret with their 2nd finger, the 2nd string on the 1st fret with the 1st finger, and play the chord while the 1st and 3rd strings are open.

The above instruction may look complicated while reading. However, applying it on the guitar will be much simpler and more straightforward. Chord diagrams that teach guitar students how to play different chords use the above numbering for strings, frets, and fingers. Therefore, understanding what these numbers represent helps guitar students to learn to play different notes and chords on the guitar.

How to Pick a Great Guitar for a Beginner

First of all, a guitar student needs to decide whether they want to buy an acoustic or electric guitar. It is true that electric guitars create a unique sound and looks much cooler. However, acoustic guitars are more recommended for beginners since the focus should be to be precise and clear with their playing, which is best accommodated by acoustic guitars. Furthermore, electric guitars feature various options that might make learning complex for beginners and confuse them.

The next step is to decide on the type of acoustic guitar that the student wants to buy. Nylon-stringed acoustic guitars are much easier to learn on since the strings have less tension. However, they are much quieter than acoustic guitars that feature steel strings. Steel rings guitars may sound louder than nylon-stringed guitars, but steel strings have more tension that can make things tough on the fingers of guitar students.

While nylon-string guitars may sound perfect for beginners, it isn't impossible to learn to play the guitar on a steel-string acoustic guitar or an electric guitar. It simply comes down to knowing the challenges associated with each of these types of guitars and committing to doing your best to overcome those obstacles with patience and persistence.

Shape and Size

The appearance of a guitar student's guitar is important. They must be proud of their guitar and want to spend more time with it. Therefore, they should purchase a guitar that they are attracted to. However, it's important to avoid picking a guitar merely based on its looks. Simply consider it as one important factor.

Pay attention to different shapes, sizes, and colors of guitars that are appealing. It's okay to check out some expensive guitars to find inspiration. There is a great chance of finding a moderately priced guitar with the same looks.

Guitars come in different sizes and shapes. As a result, they may sound different. The size and shape of a guitar also determine how easy it is to play it. Check out guitars of different body sizes and shapes. Try larger-bodied guitars create loud and thick sounds while smaller ones are less loud. Some guitars feature a body cutaway while others don't give less access to the upper frets.

It's important to sit down with a guitar and see how it feels. If it is too large and the student can't comfortably hold the fingerboard and strum, a smaller guitar is recommended.

The thickness of the guitar is also another important factor to look into. The thicker a guitar, the longer a guitarist's arms need to be to reach the strumming area and the fingerboard comfortably. Thinner bodied guitars are recommended for guitar students that practice while being seated.

Those who have compact bodies and children have the option of buying small-scale guitars. They have shorter fretboards, so there is no need to stretch to reach certain frets. The strumming hand can also be operated comfortably and naturally.

Decide a Budget

It's important to decide how much a guitar student is willing to spend on their first guitar. They must remember that it's their "first guitar," not their last. Therefore, buying a very expensive guitar is not required and recommended. However, that does not mean that beginners are better off purchasing a cheap guitar.

Cheap guitars do more harm to guitar students than good. They are likely to sound bad and make playing the guitar a painful experience for beginners. As a result, guitar students with cheap guitars are likelier to quit. Similarly, purchasing an expensive guitar may result in the student treating it as if it's made of glass. A guitar student should be able to explore the guitar. They may not know how to properly take care of a guitar while playing, storing, and transportation. Therefore, it is highly recommended that beginners pick a moderately priced guitar instead of cheap or expensive options.

Meet the Guitar in Person

Most beginners start with a low budget. As a result, many of them are encouraged to shop online as they can find guitars for cheaper prices compared to guitar shops. However, purchasing a guitar online or without personally seeing it involves many risks.

How a guitar feels is a very important part of picking the perfect guitar. Ordering online or asking someone else to purchase a guitar does not give beginners the luxury of feeling the guitar before they purchase it. It is highly recommended that guitar students take the time to meet and feel different guitars before they buy one. Doing so helps them avoid the disappointment of buying a guitar that simply doesn't feel right.

Guitar Accessories

Some guitars come with essential accessories. Others do not, and such accessories need to be purchased separately. Most guitar shops offer Starter Packs at very reasonable rates so that beginners have everything that they need to learn to play the guitar successfully.

Starter packs usually include extra strings, plectrums or picks, capos, guitar tuners, and guitar straps. Starter packs for electric guitars include amplifiers and cables. Some beginners may not have the budget to invest in a starter pack. If that's the case, they can only purchase the accessories that are essential for beginners. They include extra strings, guitar picks, and a guitar strap if they are planning to practice while standing.

Maintaining the guitar is an important activity that helps guitar students bond with their guitar and ensures that it is well and safe. Therefore, it is advised to invest in some cleaning fluid and cleaning cloths to keep their guitars clean and shiny. Accessories such as capos and slides can be purchased later, usually when they reach the intermediate level.

Chapter 4: Tuning the Guitar

One of the most important lessons of learning to play the guitar involves tuning the guitar. Guitars are stringed instruments that rely on the specific tensions of their strings to create sounds. The changes in the temperature cause guitar strings to slightly change their length, and that results in guitars falling out of tune. Guitars that are out of tune create notes and chords that are off-key.

Beginners may not realize that their guitar is out of tune and continue to practice. As a result, they may train their minds with off-key notes and chords that can hamper their growth. Therefore, it's very important to tune the guitar. It's recommended that guitar students tune their guitars before they start practicing and also store guitars in areas that do not expose them to significant variations of temperature.

How to Tune a Guitar with an Electric Tuner

Electric tuners are very straightforward to use. As a result, they are highly recommended for beginners. An electric tuner picks up the sound created by a string and displays the note that it identifies. They usually indicate whether the string is too high or too low. If the string is too high, it needs to be loosened. If it is too low, it needs to be tightened. As a string is loosened or tightened, it is played in intervals to check whether the string is in tune or getting closer to being in tune.

Electric guitar tuners come in many varieties. Some are small external devices that fit in a pocket. Some tuners can be clipped on to the guitar. Some guitars come with built-in tuners. In the digital era, a range of guitar tuning apps has also emerged. These devices may look different. However, they function in similar ways. Therefore, using these different types of tuners are very similar and straight forward.

Tuning a Guitar by Ear

This is the old-fashioned way of tuning that guitar without the use of any other external devices. It is a useful method to learn even for beginners as it does not require guitar students to have an electronic guitar tuner handy whenever they need to tune their guitars.

First, the low E string is tuned by ear. The 6th string is the thickest of strings and is highly likely to go out of tune significantly. Furthermore, most guitarists are familiar with the correct pitch of the 6th string. Beginners can get used to the correct pitch of the 6th string by practicing this method along with an electronic guitar tuner.

Once the low E string is in tune, it is fretted at the 5th fret and plucked with the right hand. It creates a note A. The 5th string, which creates an A note when plucked openly, can be tuned using the above tone. The A string or the 5th string is tightened or loosened until both the strings produce the same tone.

Once the A string (5th) is in tune, it is fretted at the fifth fret creating a note D. This tone can be used in the same way explained above to tune the 4th string or the D string. Once the D string is in tune, it is held down at the 5th fret creating a G note. This tone is used to tune the 3rd or G string.

Once the G string (3rd) is in tune, it is held at the fourth fret to create a B tone. The 2nd or B string can be tuned by using this tone as a guide. Once the B string is in tune, it is fretted at the 5th fret creating a high E tone. The high E string (1st) can be tuned using this tone as a guide.

Guitar Tuning Tips

It is natural for guitars to go out of tune. However, it can be minimized with the correct use of the guitar and the way it is handled and stored. Below are some essential guitar tuning tips for beginners. Learning to follow these tips makes guitar tuning easier and prevents guitar students from playing with a guitar that is out of tune.

Tune the Guitar Regularly

It is highly recommended that guitar students develop the habit of tuning their guitars before they start playing. Guitars can quickly go out of tune. Practicing with an out-of-tune guitar does a lot of harm in the musical sense of beginners. Therefore, guitar students must make it a habit to tune their guitars every time they play.

Store Guitars Away from Hot and Cold Places

Temperature affects the wooden body of the guitar and its strings. Therefore, storing a guitar in hot or cold places can result in it going out of tune. This can be avoided to a high degree by avoiding keeping the guitar exposed to the sun or leaving it inside hot cars. It's also important to keep guitars away from heat sources such as fireplaces and heaters. Cold wind can also cause guitars to go out of tune. Therefore, it's important to store them away from the cold wind in cold climes.

Loosen the Strings When Done

One of the best ways to enable a guitar to cope with the variations in temperature and humidity is by loosening its strings before storing or transporting it. Shaking the guitar can also make it go out of tune. Therefore, it's important to avoid bumps and falls when a guitar is being transported.

Replace Guitar Strings Regularly

Guitar strings age with time. They can get dirty, over-stretched, and corroded, making them more difficult to tune. Therefore, changing guitar strings regularly helps guitarists keep their guitars in tune. Newer strings also improve the sound that is made by a guitar. Therefore, make sure that the guitar strings are replaced as soon as they start to show signs of wear and tear.

Chapter 5: Power Chords

Anyone who has closely watched rock guitarists play may have noticed or at least gotten a glimpse of power chords at work. These chords are only made up of the root and the fifth of the particular chord. As a result, power chords do not have a major or minor quality to them. Power chords are popular in most genres. However, they are widely used by rock guitarists.

Power chords are also known as "Fifth Chords" since they use the fifth note of each chord along with its root. They have a more crunchy sound. Power chords only use three notes, making them easy to understand and play.

The wide use of power chords in rock music with guitarists playing electric guitars might mislead beginners to believe that power chords are only for electric guitars. However, power chords sound great on an acoustic guitar. Watching acoustic versions of most rock songs will help upcoming guitarists observe how they are played on acoustic guitars while sounding great.

The concept of root notes applies to almost everything that does not involve open strings on the guitar. Such scales and chords that do not use open strings can move up and down the neck of the guitar easily and play different scales and chords. The easiest way to identify and understand the chord being played along the neck of the guitar is to understand the root note of each chord.

Take the power chord C, for example. It's made of the notes C (the root) and G (the fifth) of the scale. Due to the use of these notes, the power chord is written as "C5" on tabs and chord charts. Similarly, the power chord G, written as G5, consists of the root note G and D (the fifth). It is possible to play power chords on different string groups. However, most guitarists prefer to use root 6 and 5 since the use of those strings for power chords add a powerful and deep sound.

Upon understanding how power chords are made, guitarists can easily maneuver the fretboard and play chords using different positioning. Power chords can be played throughout the neck of the guitar as well. However, playing power chords beyond the 8th fret becomes more difficult, especially for beginners, as frets are located very close to each other.

Terminology

There are divided opinions on whether power chords should be considered actual "chords" in a traditional sense. Some musicians argue that there should be at least three degrees of the scale to create a chord. Therefore, they argue that power chords are actually dyads since the same interval is found in them.

However, many musicians accept the term "power chord" as a rock and pop music term, especially when it comes to overdriven electric guitar styles that feature in punk rock, heavy metal, hard rock, and other similar genres. The term "power chord," as a result, has made its way to the vocabularies of synthesizer and keyboard players.

The most common notation used for power chords is either "5" or "(no 3). For example, a power chord with the root G is denoted as G5 or G(no 3). The first denotation simply means the root G and the fifth, while the second means that the root G without the presence of a third. "Ind" is another notation used for power chords that means "indeterminate." The term has been used to denote power chords since they are neither major nor minor.

History of Power Chords

The use of power chords by popular musicians dates back to the 1950s. Willie Johnson and Pat Hare, who played for Sun Records, are considered to be the guitarists by whom the use of power chords originated. "How Many More Years" by Howlin' Wolf with Johnson playing the guitar and "Cotton Crop Blues" by James Cotton with Hare on the guitar prove their use of power chords in the 1950s. Later in the same decade, Scotty Moore used power chords to open Jailhouse Rock by Elvis Presley with power chords.

When it comes to mainstream rock and roll artists, Link Wray is believed to be the first with his use of power chords in "Rumble" that was recorded in 1958. In 1964, The Kinks released "You Really Got Me,", which was a smash hit peaking to number seven on North American Billboard Charts. It is recognized as the first pop song to use power chords and the song that laid the foundation for power chords in mainstream and contemporary music.

The 1960s saw a counterculture in the music scene along with acid experimentation. It resulted in the expansion of sounds and textures that artists created as well as advancements in studio technology. Inspired by these changes, bands such as Pink Floyd started pushing the limits in recording while laying revolutionizing traditional music composition. The Who used power chords in their hit Baba O'Riley in 1971. It became an anthem for musical and cultural progressive ideologies.

Three years later, the Ramones pioneered the punk rock style along with performances emphasizing on aggression and raw emotion compared to technical ability and musical skill. Power chords made guitar music composing much easier, which resulted in many bands entering the music scene. Many credit the Ramones with the exponential growth of the number of bands consisting of amateur musicians. The new youth counterculture took a liking to hardcore punk due to its raw sound.

US artists such as Ozzy Osbourne and British bands such as The Who sounded more edgy and aggressive into the 1980s. This influenced the inception of heavy metal. Many heavy metal acts emerged throughout the 1980s, offering exemplary live performances and farcical off-stage antics.

The LA band NOFX was a band inspired by the Ramones with style and attitude being favored over musical ability. Their music featured simple harmonies and melodies, while the lyrical content featured humor and sarcasm that resulted in making their music highly contagious. The '90s saw the emerging of one of the most influential rock bands in the history of music: Nirvana. "Smells Like Teen Spirit" not only peaked at number one on the Billboards Charts but also inspired a new generation of youth filled with frustration and anger.

While a lot was going on in the punk scene in the 1990s, a new style was slowly emerging, spearheaded by artists such as Kid Rock. A new American genre was born inspired by the hip-hop culture and aggressive rock n' roll music. The dawning of the new millennia saw numerous indie bands striving to bring their styles into the mainstream audiences. Weezer was a band that succeeded in doing so with humorous lyrics and an iconic "nerdy" image.

Two decades into the new millennium, it is safe to say that the rebellious reputation of power chords is only going to improve and that it's definitely here to stay. Power chords are starting to push more and more into mainstream music, with many upcoming musicians being inspired by artists and bands who introduced power chords into mainstream music and revolutionized it.

Techniques

Power chords feature very close matching of overtones. This is because they are often played within a single octave. However, octave doubling is sometimes performed when playing power chords. Power chords often take a middle register pitch with their denotations, indicating the different voicing that is used. Guitarists mustn't confuse these letter names with chord names that are usually used in popular music such as C Major, G Major, B Minor, etc.

1-5 perfect fifth (A) is one such common voicing. A common octave is often added to it, creating 1-5-1 (B). Similarly, 5-1 (C) is a perfect fourth power chord and implies that the lower 1 pitch is "missing." One or both pitches can be doubled an octave below or above, which is 5-1-5-1 or is D. 5-1-5 is another common variation.

Spider Chords

This guitar technique became popular in the thrash metal scene in the '80s pioneered by the Megadeth guitarist, co-founder, and lead vocalist, Dave Mustaine. The name "Spider Chords" was given to the technique since it used four fingers of the fretting hand, giving the hand the appearance of the limbs of a spider.

Spider Chords are popular as they reduce string noise, especially when it comes to playing fast riffs with chords across multiple strings. Some good examples of the use of Spider Chords are "Holy Wars... The Punishment Due", "Wake Up Dead," and "Ride the Lightning."

Spider Chords simply enable guitarists to play two power chords without having to shift., which means they make code transition much easier and quicker. More importantly, they avoid string noise. Furthermore, the technique also provides guitarists access to a major 7th code without the 3rd. Guitarists find it easy to run up and down the neck using Spider Chords.

Beginner level guitarists may find it difficult to play Spider Chords at the beginning since all four fingers of the fretting hand may not move as equally fast in tandem. Most beginners start with playing open chords where the use of the fourth finger or "the pinky" is minimal and, at times, optional. Therefore, while they may later be able to move their first three fingers quickly, the fourth may be slower than the rest. This makes it difficult for beginners to play power chords.

However, that does not mean Spider Fingers are only for the pros. The fourth finger can be trained with constant practice. Beginner level guitarists can practice the fourth finger or the pinky by first playing open chords that use all four fingers even though the use of the fourth finger may be optional. Some good examples are the C Major and G Major chords. Once such a guitarist is confident about the movement of the four fingers of the fretting hand, they can easily learn and practice Spider Chords and experience their unique sound and mobility.

Fingering

It's safe to say that the most common implementation of power chords is the 1-5-1' form that features the root note, a fifth note above the root, and the note of the octave above the root. The lowest note is played on a particular fret on a particular string, and the other two higher notes are usually played two frets higher on the next two strings when the guitar is in standard tuning. Most guitarists play power chords using the low E string and A string for the root note. The remaining two notes are typically played using the third and fourth fingers.

Take the F power chord or F5, for example. The root note is played with the first finger on the first fret, and on the low E string. The third finger holds down the A string on the third fret, and the fourth finger is used to hold down the D string on the third fret. Sliding the same finger positioning to the third fret creates the G power chord or G5. The first finger holds down E string on the third fret. The third and fourth fingers hold down A and D strings respectively on the fifth fret.

It is important to understand that the note that is usually held by the first finger is the root note. It is the note that determines, which power chord that is being played. For example, the power chord D denoted as D5 features the root note D by holding down the A string with the first finger on the 5th fret while the third and fourth fingers hold down D and G strings on the seventh fret.

Power chords sound great when they are played correctly. Just like most other guitar chords, they take some time to perfect. Power chords require guitarists to use the fourth finger, which is often unused when playing open-string chords. Most such chords may have variations where the use of the fourth finger is optional. Therefore, some beginners may find playing power chords difficult at first since the fourth finger is likely to move slowly.

However, with practice, it will become as mobile and firm as the other three fingers. Therefore, it's important that beginners be patient when learning and playing power chords. Beginners can also avoid such difficulties by using the fourth finger from the early stages of guitar learning.

Palm-muting is another important aspect of playing power chords correctly. It's a technique that enables guitar players to mute strings as they wish. Since power chords involve strings that better not ring out for them to sound great, palm muting is an important skill a guitarist needs to develop. The absence or poor palm muting usually results in power chords sounding garbled and too loud.

Some guitarists, especially beginners, barre the second and third notes that helps them play power chords only with the use of first and third fingers. While this method may make it easier for guitarists to play power chords, using three fingers to play power chords is preferred and recommended since it provides a better finger position to change chords quickly.

Furthermore, power chords sound much better when played using three fingers instead of playing with two by barring. Therefore, it is strongly advised that beginners do not learn to play power chords using the above method. The middle finger or the second finger is usually kept idle when playing power chords unless the guitarist is playing Spider Chords.

Therefore, it's important to position the idle second finger in a comfortable position without it interfering with the position and movement of the other three fingers. Some players pull the second finger more towards the thin strings. However, it is recommended not to do so since it limits the movement of the remaining fingers and even holds down other strings without the guitarist being aware. The technique is usually used by guitar teachers merely so that the students have better visibility of the positioning of the other three fingers.

Chapter 6: Open Chords: Major Scale

Chords that include strings that are un-fretted or not held down are known as open chords. Since they include one or more open strings, they are the easiest chords that guitar students can learn to play the guitar. Some open chords include as few as two fretted strings. For example, the E Minor chord involves holding down two strings, while the remaining four strings are played open.

Learning a few open chords located on the first four frets (also known as the first position) is one of the simplest goals that guitar students can achieve. Doing so provides them the practice they require to train their fingers and be motivated by being able to play chords. The fact that many popular songs can be played using open strings also enables guitar students to start applying what they learn and become motivated from a very early stage in guitar learning.

Major Triad defines Major Chords. It is made of three notes that are spaced at different intervals in the ascending order, which is the root, major third, and perfect fifth. When these three notes are played in combination, they result in creating a happy sound. As a result, major chords feature upbeat, cheerful, and happy music.

Terminology

The open major chords are usually denoted by using the capital letters by themselves or the capital letters followed by the word "Major" although rare. When someone tells a guitarist to play an A chord, it is assumed that the chord is a major chord.

History and Famous Uses

Open position major chords have been in existence for centuries. Their exact origins are not known and may date back to the early days of the guitar. Open position major chords are used in many different genres due to the fuller and upbeat sound they create, especially in pop and other similar genres.

Techniques

Guitar students need to ensure that they develop a correct technique when playing open chords to ensure that they are not unintentionally holding down or muting any open strings. The hand needs to be arched and fingers curled to avoid such problems.

Furthermore, students are advised to make sure that they hold down the strings with their fingertips instead of the other areas of their fingers. This may be uncomfortable and at times painful for beginners who haven't developed finger callus yet. However, those discomforts will subdue with time.

Fingering

The open position (the first four frets) includes six common major chords, which are A, C, D, E, F, and G. Playing these chords on a standard-tuned guitar is easy. The most difficult of these six chords are G Major, C Major, and F Major. However, they can also be mastered with some extra practice.

E Major

The open E Major only requires a guitarist to hold down three strings while the remaining three strings are played while they are open. The chord can be played by holding down the fifth string on the second fret with the second finger, holding down the fourth string on the second fret with the third finger, and holding down the third string on the first fret with the first finger. All six strings should be strummed with them ringing out clearly.

If a muffled or dull sound is created when playing the E Major chord, guitarists must check their finger positioning to check if they are unintentionally muting any strings. Furthermore, it's important to make sure that all three strings that need to be held down are correctly and firmly held down in the right positions.

A Major

The open A Major chord is created by playing A, C#, and E notes in unison. It's important not to strum the low E (E 6th) string when playing the A Major as it affects the tone of the chord. The first variation of the A Major involves holding down the fourth, third, and second strings on the second fret with the first, second, and third fingers. Some students may find playing this version of the A Major chord difficult as it involves holding down three strings on the same fret, especially those who have thick fingers.

D Major

The open D Major chord can be played by holding down the third string on the second fret with the first finger, first string on the second fret with the second finger, and the second string on the third fret with the third finger. It's important not to strum the fifth and sixth strings when playing the D Major chord.

G Major

There are two main ways to play the open G Major chord. One of them involves three fingers, while the other involves four. The three-finger version can be played by holding down the sixth string on the third fret with the second finger, the fifth string on the second fret with the first finger, and the first string on the third fret with the fourth finger. This version is favored by many beginners as it makes it easier for them to change to the open C Major chord.

For those who are yet to develop dexterity on their fourth finger, the G Major chord can be played with the first three fingers of the left hand, with the third finger being used to hold down the first string on the third fret instead of the fourth finger. It's also a good technique to play the G Major chord on guitars with smaller necks or guitarists with smaller hands.

The four-finger version of the open G Major chord creates a more stable sound. It can be played by holding down the sixth string on the third fret with the second finger, the fifth string on the second fret with the first finger, the second and first strings on the third fret with the third and fourth fingers respectively.

C Major

The open C Major chord can be played in a few ways. However, two of those are preferred by most guitarists because they are easy to play, and because of the voicings they create. Furthermore, it's important to remember that the sixth string should not be rung when playing the C Major chord.

The open C Major chord can be played by holding down the second string on the first fret with the first finger, the fourth string on the second fret with the second finger, and the fifth string on the third fret with the third finger. The other variation additionally holds the first string on the third fret with the fourth finger.

F Major

The open F Major chord is one of the most challenging open chords for beginners. The first fingers need to be held down using the pad of the first finger creating a small barre. Both these strings must be held down firmly as failing to do so results in the strings not ringing out properly. Then the third string is held down on the second fret with the second finger, and the fourth string is held down on the third fret with the third finger. Remember not to play the fifth and sixth strings when playing the open F Major chord.

Chapter 7: Open Chords: Minor-Scale

Open position minor chords are usually played along with open position major chords when playing songs. Therefore, beginners must learn to play minor chords, especially while mixing them up with different major chords. A minor chord includes a root note, a minor third, and a fifth. The word "minor" is used to describe minor chords as they sound "lesser" compared to major chords. However, it's important to highlight the fact that their importance when playing the guitar isn't any "less" compared to other chords.

Open position minor chords, along with open position major chords, make up two of the most important guitar lessons for guitar students. They often feature songs making them highly important for beginners so that they can progress to playing more difficult chords.

Terminology

Minor chords are defined by Minor Triad. A minor triad consists of a root note, a minor third, and a perfect fifth. For example, the C minor triad consists of the notes C, Eb (E Flat), and G. Minor triads are usually represented by integer notation.

Intervals can also be used to describe a minor triad. A minor triad has a minor 3rd interval on the bottom and a major 3rd on top that acts as the root note. When comparing minor triads and major triads, minor triads feature a minor third on top, and major triads feature a major third on the bottom.

Minor chords are easy to build. First, start by holding a major chord. Doing so requires the guitarist to identify the 1st, 3rd, and 5th notes. Then, a minor chord can be built by moving the

3rd note further down the fretboard by one fret, which is equal to a half step.

For example, the C, E, and G are the 1st, 3rd, and 5th notes in the C major scale. Holding these notes create an open position C major chord. Then, move the third note, which is note E a half a step or one fret down, which is a flat or lowered third. As a result, the E note becomes an Eb (E flat).

Minor chords are usually denoted by writing the capital letter of the chord they represent, followed by a simple "m." For example, the E minor chord is denoted as "Em." Some diagrams may use the word "minor" after the capital letter of the chord. For example, the E minor chord is denoted as "E minor." Such notation is usually used for minor seventh, minor ninth, minor eleventh, and minor thirteenth categories. For example, an E minor seventh chord is denoted by "E minor 7th".

History and Famous Uses

Major chords were played as triads in Western classical music between 1600 and 1820. Later the same method was followed in pop, rock, and folk music. The minor triad is a basic tonal music building block along with the major triad. Minor chords are commonly used along with major chords, with the minor chords creating a darker sound than major chords. However, they are considered to be highly stable consonants and do not require resolution.

Techniques

Learning to play open position minor chords comfortably and correctly puts guitar students on the verge of playing simple songs on the guitar. Just like major chords, minor chords are usually easier to learn and play compared to most other chords. However, it's very important to develop the correct technique when learning to play open position minor chords.

Just like with major chords, minor chords include open strings that should not be held down when playing those chords. However, there is a chance of beginners unintentionally holding down strings that are supposed to be open when playing minor chords. Such problems can be avoided by training themselves to play with a technique that involves arched hands and curled fingers.

Some beginners hold down strings using the face of their fingers instead of fingertips, which is a technique that must be avoided at all times. Most such incorrect techniques are developed due to the discomfort experienced by beginners as their finger calluses take time to develop. However, it's important to stick to the correct technique, which is by holding down strings using the fingertips, although it may be painful in the early stages.

Fingering

The number of minor chords that can be played in the open position is limited. Open position minor chords are E minor, A minor, and D minor. If a guitar student wants to learn to play songs that include other minor chords such as F minor, G minor, and C minor, they should first learn to play barre chords.

E Minor

The open position E minor chord is one of the easiest minor chords. All strings are strummed when playing an E minor chord. An open position E minor chord can be played by simply holding down the 5th string on the 2nd fret with the 2nd finger and the 4th string on the 3rd fret with the 3rd finger.

A Minor

The open position A minor chord is also fairly simple, although it requires the guitarist to hold down three strings. It's also important to remember not to ring the 6th string when playing the chord. An open position A minor chord can be played by holding down the 2nd string on the 1st fret using your 1st finger, the 4th string on the 2nd fret using your 2nd finger, and the 3rd string on 2nd fret using your 3rd finger.

D Minor

The open position D minor chord is another essential minor chord that beginners should invest in learning. Remember not to play the 5th and 6th strings when playing the chord. The three-finger variation of the D minor chord can be made by holding down the 1st string on the first fret with the 1st finger, the 3rd string on the 2nd fret with the 2nd finger, and the second string on the 3rd fret using your 3rd finger.

B Minor

The open position B minor chord is slightly difficult compared to other open position minor chords since it requires four fingers. Just like with the D minor chord, the 5th and 6th strings are not played when playing the chord. An open position B minor chord can be played by holding down the first string on the second fret using the 1st finger, the 2nd string on the third fret with the 2nd finger, 4th string on the 4th fret with the 3rd finger, and the 3rd string on the 4th fret with the last finger.

Chapter 8: Barre Chords

A type of guitar (or other string instruments) chords is known as barre chords. They are also known as "Bar Chords" or "Barr Chords." Barre chords are played with one or more fingers pressing down multiple strings across a particular fret of the fingerboard as if the strings are being held down by a bar. It is a technique that is popular among many guitarists for a number of reasons.

One of the main reasons why guitarists use barre chords is the fact that they pave the way for chords that aren't restricted by the tones that the open strings create. For example, when a guitar is tuned to regular pitch, the open strings are E, A, D, G, B, and E. Therefore, the guitarist needs to play chords that are based on one or many of those notes if he or she plays open chords. However, barre chords do not require that. A guitarist can easily play an F# chord by barring strings, although it may not be based on any notes of the strings.

Barre chords are also "moveable,"which means the same finger positioning can be slid up and down the fretboard to play different chords. As a result, many guitarists find barre chords to be highly convenient, especially when playing riffs featuring fast chord transitions. Barre chords are heavily used in both classical and popular music as a result.

It is common to see barre chords being used alongside open chords, although there are clear differences in their tone quality. Open chords have better tone quality, while barre chords have slightly poorer tone quality in comparison. Nevertheless, the unique sounds of barre chords are frequent in pop and rock music.

Barre chords often do the job that a capo does without much fuss. A guitarist can play and open chord and then proceed to play a chord that is a number of steps higher by using barre chords. For example, if a guitarist plays an E major chord, they can easily proceed to play an F# Major by sliding the same finger positioning while barring with the first finger two frets down.

Most beginners find playing barre chords difficult. Playing barre chords require guitarists to press down multiple strings with a single finger, which is usually the first finger. Doing so can be fairly difficult for many beginner-level guitarists for a number of reasons. Therefore, mastering barre chords and playing them for prolonged periods of time takes a lot of practice.

Terminology

Barre chords are usually denoted with the use of either of the two English letters "B" or "C" followed by an Arabic or Roman numeral that indicates the position of the barre chord. For example, barre chord B that is played on the third fret is denoted by BIII or B3. Similarly, the barre chord C played on the seventh fret is denoted by either CVII or C7.

The two English letters that are used to denote barre chords stand for "barre" or "bar" and "cejillo" or "capotasto." The latter Spanish and Italian terms stand for "capo." The choice of these denotations is purely up to the editor. However, Roman numerals are preferred to denote barre chords as the use of Arabic numerals can lead to confusion between barre chords and other common chord symbols.

Partial barres are also indicated in a few ways. One of the most common methods of denoting a partial barre is by using a vertical strike through the English letter "C." However, the method does not dictate the number of strings that should be barred. Therefore, it is up to the guitarist to determine how many strings he or she is going to barre when following such denotations.

Other styles use fractions to indicate the number of strings that need to be barred, such as 1/2 and 4/6, as well as the letters B or C. The letters are completely omitted in some denotations such as classical staff notation. For example, VI4 indicates the guitarist to barre on the sixth fret over the highest four strings, which are D, G, B, and E.

History and Famous Uses

There is no clear evidence about when exactly barre chords were invented. Guitarists have been playing barre chords for centuries and using the full length of the fretboard to play different chords at different pitches. Barre chords are more prominent in rock music, although they are used by guitarists of other genres as well.

Techniques

Barre chords are often utilized to play chords that are higher in terms of position on the guitar. The choice of key is usually the primary reason that requires the use of barre chords as the particular key may not enable the guitarist to play certain open-string chords that are usually played on a standard-tuned guitar.

The most common barred fingering shapes are the ones that are used to play the open chords A and E. An A-type barre chord consists of A chord finger positioning (X02220) that can be moved up and down the fretboard while the first finger is used to barre. The positioning is also known as a "double bar" since it can be played with two fingers barring high E and A strings (first finger) and the other barring B, G, and D (third or fourth finger) while the low E string is deadened with the first finger. Second, third, and fourth fingers can also be used to hold down B, G, and D strings.

When the A chord finger positioning is barred on the second fret (X24442), it produces a B chord. It involves the first finger barring the high E (1st) and A strings while deadening the low E (6th) string on the second fret. The B, G, and D strings can be either barred on the fourth fret using the third or fourth finger or the second, third, and fourth fingers can be used to hold down the same strings. A-type positioning creates Bb, B, C, C#, D, Eb, E, F, F#, G, and Ab from fret one to eleven. The twelfth fret creates an A chord that is an octave up.

In addition to the above two common shapes, barre chords can be played using other chord fingerings. However, the player must be able to finger the chord in such a way that the first finger is idle for barring, and the chord does not need the fingers to be positioned across more than four frets.

CAGED System

The acronym CAGED stands for C, A, G, E, and D chords. It is often used to describe the use of barre chords that are free to be played anywhere on the fretboard. The acronym is used by guitar teachers and students to teach and remind the open chords that can be played as barre chords along the fretboard. Therefore, using the first finger to barre, chord shapes C, A, G, E, and D chords can be used to create barre chords anywhere on the fretboard as a guitarist wishes to play different chords in any key.

Partial Barre Chords

A complete barre chord is known as a "Great Barre," or a "Grand Barre" chord and incomplete or partial barre chords are known as "Small Barre" chords. Guitarists do find playing the F chord using the small barre chord much easier. However, doing so does not contribute to developing the technique and skill to play Great Barre chord formations. Partial or simplified barre chord versions can usually be played with the use of the first three fingers. Most guitarists find them useful when playing guitar solos.

Diagonal Barre Chord

These barre chords are very rare. They require the guitarist to barre multiple strings with the first finger on different frets. Therefore, the first finger is placed at an angle giving the impression of a diagonal. Playing diagonal barre chords require a lot of practice playing barre chords. Furthermore, most guitarists may not need to use diagonal barre chords most of the time.

Fingering

Almost every guitar student finds playing barre chords difficult. They put significant strain on the fingers and palm making them painful for beginners. However, just like every other type of guitar chords, barre chords can be mastered eventually with regular practice. What is important is to keep practicing while taking quick breaks to rest the fingers and palm. Soon enough, barre chords will start sounding great and correct.

One Finger Barre

A great exercise that is highly recommended for students learning to play barre chords is One Finger Barre. The method involves barring all the six strings with the first finger. The other fingers are kept idle. Start playing each string separately while making sure that each string is barred properly.

Then, start playing all the strings at once by strumming. Use single downward strums first. Then proceed to play upward strums and finally both to a beat. When a guitar student is able to barre correctly using the first finger, they can proceed to the next level of exercises.

Two Finger Barre

One of the factors that make barre chords difficult for beginners is the effort it requires the guitar player to put on the finger that is used to barre, which is usually the first finger. The finger needs to be held firm enough to barre the required strings. Beginners may not have enough strength on their first finger when starting to play barre chords. Therefore, they can support the first finger by barring with two fingers.

The second finger is placed on top of the first finger to barre strings when playing barre chords. Due to the extra support provided by the second finger, many beginners find this method helpful. However, a two-finger barre leaves only two more fingers for fretting. Therefore, it limits students from playing some barre chord patterns. Therefore, the technique is only prescribed when beginners are practicing barre chords. They should ideally be able to barre with just one finger eventually.

Thumb Support

What most beginners fail to do is to provide enough support for the first finger to barre by using the thumb. The thumb can be placed firmly behind the guitar's neck. It results in the first finger having more support that helps it barre strings more comfortably.

Hand Strength

How easy a beginner overcomes the obstacle of playing barre chords also depends on their hand strength. Guitar students with stronger hands usually master barre chords easily. Therefore, it's important to do some hand strengthening exercises on the guitar every day.

Hold the Guitar Correctly

Most guitar students are largely focused on their fingers and palms when playing barre chords that they forget to pay enough attention to posture and holding the guitar properly. The way that a guitarist holds the guitar determines how much support the fretting hand is going to receive from their posture. Holding the guitar correctly pushes the fretboard towards the fingers, instead of the guitarist having to push his or her fingers hard on to the fretboard.

Prioritize the Strings that Need to Ring Out

It's important to understand the strings that need to be barred when playing chords. Some strings may be held down by other fingers higher up the fretboard. Therefore, they do not need to be held down as hard. However, some strings need to be barred. Focusing on those strings by focusing pressure on barring them is often a successful approach.

For example, when holding an Am shape barre chord, the first finger barres the first five strings. However, the B, G, and D strings are held down further up the fretboard. Therefore, there is no need to barre those strings. Only E and D strings need to be prioritized. Since the E first is a thin string, it's very easy to barre it. Therefore, the player can put more pressure to barre the D string to correctly play the barre chord.

Play Lots of Power Chords

Power chords are great when it comes to strengthening the wrists of guitarists. However, they aren't as difficult as barre chords. Therefore, playing more power chords can be used as a stepping stone to playing barre chords. When a guitar student can comfortably hold power chords for five to ten minutes continuously, they are considered ready to progress to learning barre chords.

Get a Better Guitar

If a guitar student continuous to find playing barre chords difficult even after weeks of focused practice, they should take a good look at their guitar. The best option is to take the guitar to someone who knows how to play the guitar well. Some cheap guitars make playing barre chords extremely difficult. Therefore, the problem may be with the guitar instead of the guitarist.

Lower the Action

The action of a guitar is the distance between the strings and the fretboard. If the action is low, it makes it easy to hold down strings. If it's high, holding down strings and playing barre chords are difficult. The action can be lowered by adjusting the height of fret wires and the saddle. If a guitar student continuous to find playing barre chords difficult, they should take their guitar to a good guitar shop that does maintenance and repair to check if the action is low enough.

Use Lighter Strings

Some brands of guitar strings are lighter than others. Lighter strings make it easier to play barre chords. Therefore, if a guitar student is finding barre chords extremely painful and difficult, they should consider purchasing a set of lighter strings.

Detune the Guitar

A cheap trick that most beginners use when they are practicing barre chords is to detune their guitars a half-step or even a full step. Doing so usually does not alter the sound dramatically. However, the trick makes it easier to play barre chords, and it can be successfully used by beginners until they develop the correct technique and hand strength to play barre chords when their guitar is in standard tune.

Practice at Fret X

The tension of the strings varies along the fingerboard. Their tension is at the highest on fret one, and it decreases as you go higher up the fretboard. Beginners can start practicing barre chords at fret X or the middle of the guitar. As they slowly improve, they can move back towards the first fret, where playing barre chords is more challenging.

Chapter 9: More Chords

Various types of chords can be played on the guitar other than open position major and minor chords, power chords, and barre chords. Although these might not be included in many songs, some songs do include chord varieties to create better-sounding music. Beginners often skip such chords while skipping to the chords they know how to play. However, reaching the intermediate level requires guitarists to comfortably play different types of guitar chords, especially those mentioned below.

Diminished Chords

This group of chords creates a tense and unpleasant sound. A diminished chord is made up of a root note, which is the 1st, a minor third, which is three semitones higher, and a flat or diminished fifth, which is six semitones higher. They serve an important purpose in music, although they aren't used very often.

For example, the C Diminished chord can be built with a C note acting as the root note. Then three semitones can be counted to find the minor 3rd, which is an Eb or D#. Six semitones need to be counted from C to locate the diminished fifth. In this case, it is Gb or F#. The C diminished chord can be played using these three notes, which are C, Eb, and Gb.

Major Seventh Chord

This group of chords creates a soft and thoughtful sound. Major seventh chords are commonly used in Jazz music. They consist of a root note, which is the 1st, a major third, which is four semitones higher, a perfect 5th, which is seven semitones higher, and a major 7th, which is eleven semitones higher. Major seventh chords are similar to major triads, with the only difference being the major 7th on top.

For example, the C major seventh chord can be built with a C note acting as the root note. Then four semitones are counted to located the major third, which is an E, and a further three semitones from there or seven semitones from the root are counted to locate the 5th. Finally, the major 7th is located by counting 11 semitones from the root C. This gives the notes C, E, G, and B, which can be played in unison to create the C major seventh chord.

Minor Seventh

This group of chords helps create a contemplative or moody sound. Major chords create a happy sound, while minor chords create a sad sound. Minor seventh chords create a sound that is somewhere in between these two moods. Minor seventh chords consist of a root note, which is the 1st, a minor 3rd located three semitones higher, a perfect 5th located seven semitones higher from the root, and a minor 7th, located ten semitones higher from the root. Similar to major seventh chords, minor seventh chords are minor triads with a minor 7th on top.

For example, building a C minor seventh chord is started by locating the root note, which is C. The minor 3rd can be located by counting three semitones from the root, which is an Eb. The perfect 5th can be located by counting seven semitones from the root, which is a G. The minor 7th can be located by counting ten semitones from the root, which is a Bb. The C minor seventh chord can be played by playing C, Eb, G, and Bb together.

Dominant Seventh

This group of chords creates a restless and strong sound. Dominant seventh chords are commonly in Blues, Jazz, Hip Hop, RnB, and EDM genres. A dominant seventh chord is built using a root note, which is the 1st, a major 3rd located four semitones higher, a perfect 5 located seven semitones higher, and a minor 7th located 10 semitones higher from the root note.

For example, it is started by locating the root note, which is C. The major 3rd can be located by counting four semitones, which gives an E note. The perfect 5th can be located by counting seven semitones from the root, which should give a G, and the minor 7th can be located by counting 10 semitones from the root, which is a Bb note. The C dominant seventh can be played by playing the C, E, G, and Bb notes together.

Suspended Chords

All different types of chords discussed in this chapter consisted of a root note, a 3rd, and a 5th. However, not all chords are made using this foundation. Suspended chords are a good example. This group of chords sounds nervous and bright. Suspended chords are denoted with the use of the term "sus."

A suspended chord is built using a root note, which is the 1st, a major 2nd, which is two semitones higher, and a perfect 5th, which is seven semitones from the root. It's also safe to say that sus2 chords are major chords with a major second in the place of the usual major third.

For example, the Csus2 chord can be built by first locating the root note, which is C, and then counting two semitones to locate the major second, which is a D note. Finally, seven semitones are counted from the root note to locate the perfect fifth, which is a G note. The Csus2 chord can be now played using the notes C, D, and G.

Sus4 chords are quite similar to sus2 chords as they also create a nervous and bright mood. A sus4 chord can be built using a root note, which is the 1st, a major four, which is five semitones higher, and a perfect fifth, which is seven semitones above the root note. It's easy to think of sus4 chords as major chords with a perfect fourth in the place of the usual major third.

For example, the Csus4 chord can be built by first locating the root note, which is C, and then counting five semitones to locate the perfect 4th, which is an F note. Finally, seven semitones are counted from the root to locate the perfect fifth, which is a G note. The Csus4 chord can now be played using the notes C, F, and G.

Augmented Chords

This group of chords creates a suspenseful and anxious mood. An augmented chord can be built using a root note, which is the first, a major third, which is four semitones higher, and an augmented 5th, which is located eight semitones higher from the root note. It's easy to think of augmented chords as major chords with the top note one semitone above than usual.

For example, the C aug can be built by first locating the root note, which is C, and then counting four semitones to locate the major third, which is E. Finally the augmented fifth is located by counting eight semitones from the root note, which in this case is a G# note. The C aug chord can now be played using the notes C, F, and G#.

Chapter 10: The Right Hand and Strumming

Guitarists should be able to strum effortlessly, and it should feel very natural to them. However, most beginners find strumming difficult, and it takes some practice until it becomes a natural motion to them. Different songs require different strumming patterns. Therefore, guitar students need to learn and practice the most common strumming patterns so that they can comfortably play different songs.

Guitar students must play actual songs to learn strumming patterns instead of doing simple exercises. It makes guitar learning more fun and efficient. Furthermore, listening to a particular strum pattern makes it easier for guitar students to learn it as it gives them an idea of how it should sound when played correctly. Developing a good technique for strumming is very important for beginners as it makes strumming effortless and comfortable for them. Furthermore, it's highly recommended that this chapter is followed with the regular application, just like most other chapters in this guide.

Getting the Rhythm into Your Head

Strumming is all about creating the correct rhythm for the particular song and maintaining it. Therefore, it's important not to focus too much on the strumming pattern. Start by listening to the particular song first and remember its rhythm. That groove needs to be maintained with strumming. It's also a good exercise to imagine how the strumming for that particular song should sound like. One of the best ways to achieve these goals is by actually singing the song. Singing the song out loud helps a guitar student to remember the rhythm that they need to create with strumming.

The Wrist Should be Relaxed

Most beginners tend to maintain very tense strumming hands as they are highly focused on maintaining the correct strumming patterns throughout a song. However, strumming should be a motion that feels very natural, and maintaining a relaxed wrist is an integral part of achieving such a natural motion.

It's important to remember that most of the motion when strumming should come from the guitarist's wrist. However, some beginners make the mistake of making a lot of movement with their arm instead of the wrist. While it's true that there will be some movement in their arms, it should be kept to a minimum with the wrist doing the bulk of the work.

Keep Things Moving

It's important to keep the strumming hand on the move when practicing strumming. It's an important exercise since it eliminates the need to make an effort to restart strumming after pausing during a song. So keep the strumming hand moving throughout a song so that it's easier to focus on maintaining the rhythm.

Don't Hit All the Chords!

Another common mistake that many beginners make is hitting all the strings while strumming. However, only three or four strings are hit with most chords. It may be difficult to remember, which strings to avoid different chords. Therefore, a good trick is to focus on the lower strings for the first and third beats and higher strings for the second and fourth beats.

Strumming Patterns

Beginners need to practice strumming with the most basic patterns and slowly progress to more difficult ones as they grow their strumming skills. As recommended earlier, it's better to practice strumming by playing different songs instead of doing boring strumming exercises.

However, if a guitar student isn't comfortable with changing chords, they may have no option other than to practice strumming while holding the chords that they know. Trying to practice with songs is not advised for students who are not comfortable playing and changing different chords yet. Furthermore, it's highly recommended that students master those skills before progressing into this chapter.

Only Down-Strums

Down-strums require the strumming hand to move downward. The beat that is the easiest to practice strumming is 4/4 that divides the music into four-beat sections. 4/4 beats are easy to understand and maintain. Practice by playing a down-strum for every beat.

Adding Up-Strums

Playing down-strums for a 4/4 beat should give a beginner some idea about what strumming requires and how it should sound like. Now it's time to add up-strums into the lesson. There are many simple songs that beginners can choose when learning to strum. However, this early in the process, they are highly recommended to play to a song that only features a single chord.

"Coconut" by Harry Nilsson and "Papa Was a Rolling Stone" by The Temptations are some good examples. Playing a simple one-chord song eliminates the need to focus on changing chords when learning to strum. Therefore, the student can solely focus on strumming.

Start adding by adding up-strums into the basic down-strum-only pattern that was suggested earlier. Focus on the difference in sounds up-strums, and down-strums create. It's an important exercise so that a guitar student knows when to play an up-strum and when to play a down-strum while playing a song. "Straight and Narrow" by Teenage Fanclub is a good song to practice this pattern.

Skipping Down-Strums

Once playing down-strums and up-strums is practiced, guitar students should learn to skip down-strums as needed to end up with a basic and correct strumming technique. At this stage, a student should be able to maintain strumming without any pauses. They must understand when to play down-strums and up-strums in a song, depending on whether it's a downbeat or an upbeat.

Start by playing different patterns that skip down-strums instead of ones that alternate between down-strums and up-strums. A simple exercise is to play a pattern that includes two back-to-back up-strums followed by a single down-strum and a single up-strum. Repeating this pattern requires the guitarist to skip a down-strum continuously. "Hey Ya!" by Outcast is a good song to practice this technique.

Keep in mind that skipping down-strums create a pause where beginners may be tempted to stop moving their strumming hand. However, as advised earlier, it's important to keep the strumming hand moving without hitting any strings.

Chapter 11: Holding the Pick and the Left-Hand Technique

The correct technique related to holding the guitar and the positioning of the left hand is very important to beginners. Holding the plectrum correctly enables guitarists to effortlessly strum while the correct left-hand technique paves the way for quick and smooth changing of chords while utilizing different areas of the fretboard.

Choosing the Right Guitar Pick

Picking the right guitar plectrum can be a confusing task for beginners. Guitar picks come in varying weights and thicknesses. There are many options when it comes to guitar picks, and beginners can get easily overwhelmed as a result. Lightweight picks are generally recommended for beginners. However, playing basic riffs and scales require a moderately weighed plectrum. Heavy picks are usually suited when playing guitar solos or when playing electric guitars.

Beginners need to start with a few lightweight picks and get a feel of them before settling to a thickness and weight that suits them the most. Transitioning to a medium weight pick should also be done with a few different options. There is no need to try heavy picks until a guitar student starts playing guitar solos. However, it does not hurt to buy a heavy pick and have a feel.

Guitar picks have the tendency to disappear. Therefore, a guitar student must invest in a few picks. Buying guitar picks in bulk is also a good option as they are quite inexpensive. So a beginner can easily start with ten or so bright-colored guitar picks that are easy to spot.

Holding a Guitar Pick Correctly

It's important to hold the guitar pick the correct way to be able to strum with it easily and in a natural motion. Relax the right hand by shaking and stretching it before picking up the plectrum. Then place the thumb on the outer surface of the index finger to form a loose fist. Hold the pick between the thumb and index finger with the thumb facing the guitar.

Approximately half an inch of the pick should be sticking out of the thumb. That's the area that is used to ring the strings when playing the guitar. It's okay to leave a larger area exposed when strumming and a lesser area exposed when picking notes. There is no need to exert a lot of pressure on the plectrum. Simply exert enough pressure to ensure that the pick does not fall during strumming or picking with the right hand as relaxed as possible.

Tapping and Slurs

This is a guitar technique that is used in many genres of music. It is simply using hammer-ons and hammer-offs (or pull-offs) with the left hand when playing notes. Hammer-ons and hammer-offs were discussed in Chapter 14. Slurs are used to denote tapping.

Fingering Notation

Learning to play the guitar requires guitar students to understand guitar-specific notation. However, it is very simple and straightforward. Fingering notation helps guitarists understand, which fingers to use to hold down strings when playing notes and chords. The most common fingering notation describes fingers using numbers. The index finger is assigned number 1, the middle finger is assigned number 2, the ring finger is assigned number 3, and the little finger is assigned number four.

Sometimes, letters are used to describe different fingers of the left hand in flamenco style and special percussive techniques. These styles and techniques also use the thumb without the use of the little finger. The letter "p," which stands for "pulgar" describes the thumb, the letter "i," which stands for "indice" describes the index finger, the letter "m," which stands for "medio" describes the middle finger, and the letter "a," which stands for "anular" describes the ring finger.

Vibrato

Vibrato is a beautiful effect that is often used by guitarists. Both fast and slow vibrato is used to create agitated, sweet, or sad moods to give music more character. Vibrato lengthens how long a note can be sustained. As a result, it adds personality and depth to a note. It is achieved by either lengthens or shortens a string with the use of a left-hand finger. Various vibrato techniques are used by guitarists.

The Radius/Ulna Vibrato

This technique is preferred by most guitarists as it allows more flexibility and freedom for the wrist and joints in the left hand. The Radius and Ulna bones of the forearm. The technique uses these bones in the motion that is similar to turning a doorknob to achieve vibrato. It is quite a difficult technique, but it can be mastered with enough practice.

The Push-Pull Vibrato

Most classical guitarists use this method to achieve vibrato. It involves pushing the string into the fret and then pulling it back from the fret. The hand also slightly moves back and forth when applying this technique. The push-pull method enables guitarists to achieve a wider vibrato that is more defined than the sound created with the radius/ulna vibrato technique.

The Rocker Vibrato

This vibrato technique is very common among steel-string and electric guitarists. It involves moving the string towards and away from the neighboring strings. The high tension of steel strings and electric guitar strings create a bending effect of the pitch. This technique may not be very practical on classical and nylon-stringed guitars as there isn't enough tension to create a significant vibrato.

Harmonics

When an open E string is played by a guitarist, it creates a sound that includes not only the fundamental note E but also a cluster of other notes due to the variations created by the string. These clusters can be dampened by lightly touching the string so that the fundamental E note is isolated. This technique is known as harmonics. They result in a purer and clearer ringing sound when an open or fretted string is played.

Harmonics are widely used by bands such as The Beatles, Led Zeppelin, U2, Metallica, and Yes. Harmonics can be categorized into two groups as natural harmonics and artificial harmonics. Natural harmonics are played on open strings while artificial harmonics are played on fretted strings. Harmonics can be created using numerous techniques.

One such common technique is the artificial harmonics technique. A fretted note is played between the first and tenth frets. Then the guitarist places the right-hand index finger lightly on the same string twelve frets higher. It's important to place the finger very lightly on the string without touching the fretboard. Then the string is plucked using the right-hand thumb with both the fingers in place. This results in the generation of a harmonic an octave higher than the note held by the left hand. Tap harmonics is another common method where a note is held with the left hand followed by the tapping of the same string with the right-hand fingers 12 frets higher up the fretboard.

Left Hand Technique

Guitar students should develop a strong and correct left-hand technique so that they find moving the fingers on the fretboard freely and comfortably. More importantly, it helps them to play the guitar more accurately. Using the right technique makes learning the guitar much easier and enjoyable for guitar students.

Start by keeping the wrist as straight as possible. Maintaining a straight wrist allows a guitarist to move their fingers along the fretboard freely. Bending the wrist limits the movement of fingers and, at times, damage the hand as it squeezes nerves and tendons. Numbness, pain, and tingling are signs of incorrect wrist positioning.

It may not be able to maintain a perfectly straight wrist, especially when playing certain chords. Therefore, it's important to highlight the fact that the wrist should be held straight "as much as possible" and not "at all times." Bending the wrist momentarily when playing is okay when playing the guitar.

The thumb should be firmly placed behind the neck. Many beginners try to place the entire padded area of the thumb on the neck. However, there is no need to do so, as playing different chords may require the thumb positioning to change slightly. The side of the thumb is preferred by many guitarists as the point of contact.

Remember to maintain a small gap between the left hand and the guitar neck. It allows easy movement of the fingers. Maintaining such a gap also allows the guitarist to make adjustments to reach the strings if required. The arm and elbow of the left hand should be focused on supporting the hand. Therefore, they should not be in a fixed position. They should be relaxed to avoid tension.

It's important to direct the pressure on the fretboard instead of other parts of the guitar. It enables guitarists to be more efficient and free when playing the guitar. Guitarists should learn to be as economical as possible when playing the guitar. Doing so allows them to change the position of the left hand effortlessly.

Chapter 12: Single Notes Patterns

Power chords indeed help guitarists create some amazingly fast and heavy riffs. However, single-note patterns are also used to play even better-sounding guitar riffs. Some great and popular uses of single-note riffs are Megadeth, Metallica, At the Gates, Children of Bodom, and In Flames. Single-note riffs utilize a variety of tonalities and scales to play the music that creates varying impressions and moods.

Playing such riffs and guitar solos require guitar students to learn guitar scales. It can be a daunting task for many beginners. However, just like anything else that is related to learning to play the guitar, scales can also be mastered with the right approach, resources, and practice. Various note patterns exist throughout the fretboard. Scales are similar patterns, and the basis behind scales is quite simple.

The concept of learning patterns involves, which fret positions, on, which strings are in the key to the accompanying chord, and which frets that need to be avoided. Playing patterns help guitar students to develop correct techniques when it comes to playing scales, especially related to the use of the correct fingers for particular frets.

Learning Guitar Scales

Most beginners don't pay attention to learning guitar scales as they are more focused on learning chords. However, it's important to remember that learning scales opens them up to playing single-note riffs. Any beginners who are hoping to play lead guitar at some point down the road should pay extra attention to learning guitar scales. Doing so will eventually enable them to play single-note melodies and solos.

Understanding music theory is also important when learning to play single-note patterns. It not only makes a student a better guitarist but also makes learning much efficient. The great thing about learning scales is the fact that it's neither too early nor too late to learn them. Therefore, beginners can focus on learning chords and then later learn to play scales and single-note patterns. However, if scales and single-note patterns appeal to a beginner more, they shouldn't think twice about starting to learn play scales.

A scale simply consists of a sequence of steps that are fixed between musical points. The two fixed points are the same note, although they are in different octaves. They are called the "root notes" of that particular scale. The steps of the scale simply create notes starting from the lower root note to the higher root note. There are numerous scale patterns. However, most guitarists only need to learn a few of them, and they should be sufficient even for intermediate guitarists.

Scale Patterns

A full octave consists of 12 notes that can be played in sequence between the lower and higher root notes. While the 1st and 12th notes are fixed, the pattern of the remaining 10 notes can be different. For example, think of an octave as a ladder. The 1st and last (12th) steps of the ladder are fixed to ensure its structural integrity. However, the middle steps can be changed.

The sequence that the middle steps are arranged in the ladder represents different scale patterns. Since there are 12 notes in an octave, there many different permutations or scale patterns that guitarists can create. Some beginners may be overwhelmed thinking about a large number of patterns that exist in an octave. However, figuring them out is quite simple.

One of the most important attributes of scale patterns is that they are movable. A guitarist can play the same pattern on the 1st string or the 5th string. However, where the scale begins dictates its tonality. If a guitarist starts playing a scale on the 5th fret, they will be playing an A major scale. If the same pattern is played on the 7th fret, it will be a B major scale.

Every scale consists of a root note, and a particular scale is named after the root note. The root note of a B major scale is B, and the root note of an E major scale is E. The root note is also known as the "hero note." The hero note usually sounds great, and most guitar solos and single-note riffs include the hero note abundantly.

The Major Scale

The major scale acts as a yardstick to, which every other chord and scale is compared to. Therefore, the best place to start learning guitar scales is the Major Scale. The Major Scale creates sounds that a happy, uplifting, and sweet.

The Minor Scale

The Minor Scale acts as a counterpoint to the major scale. Understanding the guitar has a lot to do with the moods its music creates. The Minor Scale sounds melancholy and sad, which is the opposite of the mood created by the major scale. However, that doesn't make the Minor Scale any less important.

Although the Minor Scale sounds sad and melancholy, it is considered to be more interesting at the same time. It also forms the foundation for the Blues Scale and Minor Pentatonic Scale, which are some of the most fun scales to learn. There are three types of Minor Scales, which are the Natural Minor Scale, the Harmonic Minor Scale, and the Melodic Minor Scale.

Guitar students must learn the Natural Minor Scale. The Harmonic Minor Scale and Melodic Minor Scale, on the other hand, are optional.

The Harmonic Minor Scale

There is only a very slight difference between the Natural Minor Scale and the Harmonic Minor Scale. The Harmonic Minor Scale sharpens the penultimate note so that the root note sounds stronger, creating a three-step interval that sounds exotic.

The Melodic Minor Scale

The three-step interval that was mentioned above isn't welcome in traditional music. Therefore, an extra note is added to smoothen the ascension creating the Melodic Minor Scale. It's also known as the Jazz Melodic Minor Scale.

Major and Minor Pentatonic Scales

The Major and Minor Scales can be considered as the pillar of music scales. Guitar students need to learn these two scales. The Major Pentatonic Scale is the abridged form of the Major Scale. Therefore, there isn't a big difference between the two scales. As a matter of fact, the Major Pentatonic Scale is a simpler form of the Major Scale. The Minor Pentatonic Scale is highly advised for beginners, especially those who aspire to play guitar solos.

Chapter 13: Open Position Scales

Learning to play Major Scales in an open position is valuable for guitars students who are either aspiring to play rhythm, lead, or try both. These guitar scales can be very useful for rhythm guitarists as understanding and knowing how to play open position major scales allow them to play single-note riffs, create new chords, and add notes to different chord voicings. Similarly, lead guitarists also benefit from learning open position major scales as it helps them improvise successfully.

Most beginners are likely to start playing the guitar as rhythm players, although they might aspire to become a lead guitarist down the road. Learning open position major scales is considered as a great way to switch from playing rhythm guitar to lead guitar.

One of the simplest methods to practice Major Scales in an open position is by starting from the low root, ascending through to the highest note and descending to the lowest root passing the original root, and finally ascending to finish on the original root. It's important to start and end on the root since it helps remember the key or the scale in the guitarist's ear.

The C Major Scale (Open Position)

The key of C major includes notes from low C to high C without any flat or sharp notes. The C Major Scale, therefore, includes C, D, E, F, G, A, B, and C notes. Start by playing the low C, which is played by holding down the fifth string on the third fret. Then, descend to the last note, which is E, by playing the sixth string open. Now, ascend to the high position, the G, located at the first string of the third fret. Finally, descend back to the low C by playing a fifth string of the third fret.

The G Major Scale (Open Position)

The key of G major includes the notes starting at G low to G high along with an F#. The G Major Scale, therefore, consists of G, A, B, C, D, E, F#, and G notes.

The D Major Scale (Open Position)

The key of D major includes notes starting at D low to D high along with F# and C#. The D Major Scale, therefore, consists of D, E, F#, G, A, B, C#, and D notes.

The open position D Major Scale has two versions. The first uses the fingers 2, 2, and 4 on the frets 2, 3, and 4, while the second version uses fingers 1, 2, and 3 on the frets 2, 3, and 4. It is a common practice to move up a position if playing a scale requires not to use the first finger on two or extra strings.

The A Major Scale (Open Position)

The key of A major includes the notes starting at A low to A hgih along with F#, C#, and G#. The A Major Scale, therefore, consists of A, B, C#, D, E, F#, G#, and A notes.

Similar to the key of D, the open position A Major Scale has two versions. The first uses the 1, 2, 3, and 4 fingers on frets 1, 2, 3, and 4. The second version shifts up a position using fingers 1, 2, and 3 on frets 2, 3, and 4. It also involves quickly shifting back to the G# note on the 3rd string at the first fret that requires the guitarist to play two back to back notes with the first finger.

The E Major Scale (Open Position)

The key of E major includes notes starting at E low to E high along with F#, C#, G#, and D#. The E Major Scale, therefore, consists of E, F#, G#, A, B, C#, D#, and E notes.

Similar to the key of D and A, the open position E Major Scale has two versions. The first one uses the 1, 2, 3, and 4 fingers at fret 1, 2, 3, and 4. The second version, on the other hand, shifts to the second position and uses fingers 1, 2, and 3 at frets 2, 3, and 4.

It also involves two shifts to the first position where the D# note is played on the 4th string at fret 1 , and the G# note is played on the 3rd string at fret 1 that requires the guitarist to play two back-to-back notes with the finger 1 on two different strings. It may feel a little difficult at the start, but it should become familiar with the practice.

Chapter 14: Articulations

Changes in rhythm, tempo, and the character of the sound can be studied when listening to music. For example, a musician may play a sequence of notes loudly, followed by some softer notes to build up to louder ones. The sense of knowing when to make such changes in sound is known as articulation in music.

Think of an actor reading lines from a script. He or she may change the tone depending on the context of the lines. In a cheerful scene, the actor will use loud and enthusiastic tones with the lines being spoken quickly. In a sad scene, he or she may read out the lines slowly in a sorrowful voice with long pauses between sentences.

When it comes to playing the guitar, the manner that a series of notes is played is known as articulation. Various marks are used to denote articulation, such as dot. It's a sign that describes a note being played as short as possible. Smoothly playing of a pitch is marked by a curved line either above or below the notes. These signs that are known as slurs are used in not only stringed instruments such as guitars but also vocal music.

Legato

The word "Legato" means "bound." It is a type of articulation that leaves almost no gap between two notes. The slur sign is used to denote Legato that calls for an unobstructed and smooth transition to the second note. Guitarists use various techniques to achieve Legato, such as pull-offs and hammer-ons, so that the second note gets a smoother start.

Hammer-Ons

One of the best ways to play Legatos is by using hammer-ons. Hammer-ons and pull-offs go hand in hand when playing the guitar. Therefore, it's important to master both techniques. The great news is that they are both very straightforward and easy techniques.

Start by holding a note down on any fret and string with the index finger. Then, pluck the note. Now the string vibrates and rings. Now, use the middle finger to sharply hold down the same string one or two frets up from where the first note was played. Doing so results in the sounding of a second note. However, the string is only plucked once. This technique is known as a hammer-on.

Any finger can be used to hammer-on depending on, which finger is used to play the first note. Furthermore, it does not matter how many frets up or down the second note is played in relation to the fret where the first note was played at. However, most hammer-ons are just a few frets apart since the reach of the fingers is limited.

Pull-Offs

A pull-off is the opposite of a hammer-on. Start by doing a hammer-on. The hammer on should leave one of the fingers on a different fret. Now, pull the finger off that fret, while making sure that the string is slightly pulled as the finger is removed. Doing so results in the string starting to ring the note that was held at the end of the hammer-on.

Hammer-ons and pull-offs do not need to be learned separately. Mastering one technique usually means that the other is already mastered. In other words, a hammer-on is naturally followed by a pull-off.

Staccato

The word "Staccato" describes a type of articulation where a note is cut short. A Staccato is indicated using a dot either above or below the notes. Sometimes the word "stacc" is used to denote a Staccato.

When a note is played on a guitar, it usually rings or continues. However, to achieve Staccatos, such as ringing or the continuation of the sound of a note needs to be dampened. Guitarists achieve this by removing the left hand unless the note is played on an open string. Some guitarists touch the vibrating string with their left hand soon after the note is played. However, it is a difficult technique, especially if other notes are to follow soon.

The most common method used by guitarists to achieve Staccatos features the right hand. The note is played, and the right hand is used to touch the string so that it stops ringing. This technique frees the left hand so that the next notes can be played without delay.

Palm-Muting

Staccato can be performed on chords using palm-muting. It is a technique that is commonly used by guitarists across various genres. Listening to palm-muting and understanding what it sounds is an important exercise for guitar students as it enables them to ensure that they palm-mute correctly. Many punk rock and metal guitarists use palm-muting with Blink 182 and Metallica being some good examples.

Palm-muting involves placing the heel of the guitarists strumming hand on the strings just as they start to ring. The hand is usually placed on the string close to the bridge of the guitar, making it easy for strumming to continue. Palm-muting can be achieved further away from the bridge as well. Therefore, it's advised that beginners try different positions of palm-muting and settle for an area that they are comfortable with.

The trickiest part of palm-muting is learning how hard or soft the hand needs to be momentarily rested on the strings when palm-muting. Palm-muting does not require the guitarist to hold down their palm on the string very hard. Only a slight or soft push on the strings is enough to mute them. Pushing too hard results in the sound completely deadening, which isn't the desired effect of palm-muting.

Chapter 15: Improvisation

Most guitar students lose focus on growing as guitarists as they become comfortable playing chords and notes. Many beginners often reach a level where they can comfortably play songs and do not work on growing as guitarists from that point on. Improvisation is one of the most important aspects of a guitarist's growth.

However, it's important to remember that growth as a guitarist is important even after reaching the intermediate level. Practicing melodic patterns, arpeggios, triads, and licks are great when it comes to sharpening a guitarist's improvisation skills. It's one of the most fulfilling aspects of playing the guitar.

When a guitar student reaches the level where he or she starts thinking about improvisation, they should know a thing or two about hard work and dedication. Improvisation requires those ingredients in abundance. It's also important for guitar students to be curious about improvisation so that they can explore, learn, and grow as guitarists.

Pentatonics / Blues Scale

The Pentatonic and Blues scale lays the foundation for playing blues, rock, pop, metal, and country solos. Therefore, guitar students must learn to play all five shapes of the Pentatonic / Blues scale. Learning this scale is a difficult task. However, it can be achieved with regular practice and hard work.

Major Scale

Learning to play the Major Scale is one of the most important lessons upon mastering the Pentatonic Scale. Guitar students must make sure that they can play the Major Scale in every position throughout the fingerboard, starting from the root note. Just like learning the Pentatonic or Blues Scale, mastering the Major Scale takes hard work and time.

Once a guitar student masters the Major Scale, they can start connecting different positions and scales. For example, a student can start by playing a part of the scale in the first position and then continue in the second position, followed by moving on to the third position. Guitar students must experiment with such different combinations so that they know the Major Scale well.

Melodic Patterns

Another type of pattern that is very useful when improvising is Melodic Patterns. These sequences and patterns help guitar students to showcase their skills with scales and give them more freedom and possibilities with their playing. Some important lessons are learning the 3rds, 4ths, 5ths, 6ths, three in a line, and 4 in a line scales.

Major Scale = 1 2 3 4 5 6 7 8 9 10 11 12 13 14 15

C Major Scale = C D E F G A B C D E F G A B C

3rds = 1 3, 2 4, 3 5, 4 6, 5 7, 6 8, 7 9, 8 10, 9 11, and so on...

C major scale = C E, D F, E G, F A, G B, A C, B D, C E, D F, and so on...

4ths = 1 4, 2 5, 3 6, 4 7, 5 8, 6 9, 7 10, 8 11, 9 12, and so on...

5ths = 1 5, 2 6, 3 7, 4 8, 5 9, 6 10, 7 11, 8 12, 9 13, and so on...

6ths = 1 6, 2 7, 3 8, 4 9, 5 10, 6 11, 7 12, 8 13, 9 14, and so on...

3 in a line = 123, 234, 345, 456, 567, 678, 789, and so on...

4 in a line = 1234, 2345, 3456, 4567, 5678, 6789, and so on...

Random Notes

Guitars students do not always need to play different scales. They should play random notes so that they learn the scales well and become more flexible and creative while enjoying a lot of freedom while improvising.

Major scale = 1 2 3 4 5 6 7 8 9 10 11 12 13 14 15

Pick out notes randomly: 1 6 3 2 12 15 3 5 11 7 etc.

Triads

Diatonic and Pentatonic Scales are great for improvisation. However, guitar students should not stop there. Learning to play triads helps guitar students grow further from playing Diatonic and Pentatonic Scales. Triads are chords that consist of three notes. There are four types of triads, which are major, minor, diminished, and augmented.

Major Scale = 1 2 3 4 5 6 7 8, C Major Scale = C D E F G A B C

Major Triad = 1 3 5, C Major Triad = C E G (= C)

Minor Triad = 1 b3 5, C Minor Triad = C Eb G (= Cm)

Augmented Triad = 1 3 #5, C Aug Triad = C E G# (= C+)

Diminished Triad = 1 b3 b5, C Dim Triad = C Eb Gb (= Co)

Students need to master all the triads in the major scale. For example, the C Major Scale consists of the following triads: C

Major Triad, D Minor Triad, E Minor Triad, F Major Triad, G Major Triad, A Minor Triad, and B Dim Triad.

Arpeggios

Guitar students can progress another step in improvisation by learning arpeggios and using that knowledge when improvising. Similar to triads, arpeggios provide more flexibility to guitarists while adding more variety to their improvisational skills. If a triad is played note by note, it is an arpeggio. However, arpeggios can be expanded while triads only contain three notes. Arpeggios can be played with maj7, b7, 9th, 11th, and more, which gives guitarists endless possibilities.

Licks

A short series of notes that can be used for improvisation to create a melodic sound is known as a lick. Guitar students should consider learning and practicing licks as an ongoing process that will grow their improvisational skills.

Modes

There are seven modes of the Major Scale. Learning to play these seven modes is a great way to improve a guitarist's improvisational skills. Below are the seven modes of the Major Scale:

Ionian = 1 2 3 4 5 6 7 8

Phrygian = 1 b2 b3 4 5 b6 b7 8

Dorian = 1 2 b3 4 5 6 b7 8

Lydian = 1 2 3 #4 5 6 7 8

Aeolian = 1 2 b3 4 5 b6 b7 8

Mixolydian = 1 2 3 4 5 6 b7 8

Locrian = 1 b2 b3 4 b5 b6 b7 8

Solos

Most beginners are inspired to learn to play the guitar by their favorite bands and artists. Therefore, it is highly likely that a guitar student has at least a few favorite guitarists. Solos are appreciated by guitar enthusiasts, and most guitar students have their favorite solos.

Learning guitar solos of a guitar student's favorite songs can help them be inspired to improvise down the road. Furthermore, the exercise helps guitar students sharpen their improvisational skills so that they can create their own guitar solos as they reach the intermediate or expert levels.

Improvise

There is no better way to learn to improvise on the guitar than to do it. A foundation indeed needs to be laid by practicing different scales and patterns so that a guitar student has the skills required to improvise. However, once a guitar student gains enough skills, he or she should be encouraged to improvise.

They may not sound great in the beginning. They may make mistakes. However, the trick is to correct those mistakes, persist, and experiment so that they can finally improvise well.

Chapter 16: Genres, Blues, World Scales, Rock, and So On

Different styles of music can be categorized into music genres. A music genre includes music that aligns with a shared tradition and sound. An artist or band belonging to a certain music genre can be distinguished by their form of music and style. Some artists and bands might belong to one music genre, while others may belong to multiple genres.

For example, some artists and bands belong to the sub-genre pop-rock, where the genres pop and rock are used interchangeably, creating a subcategory of sorts. There are tens of music genres in the world. However, the number of popular music genres is limited, with most musicians and music students having a very good understanding of what they are and how to distinguish them and their differences.

Blues

This genre of music originated in the Deep South of the United States in the 1870s. Blues genre has its roots in the traditions of African music having been originated in the African-American communities in America. Blues include spirituals and work songs, including various field hollers, chants, shouts, and simple ballads.

The term "Blues" may have been originated from "Blue Devils," which is a term used in George Colman's Search Blue Devils: A Farce, in One Act, referring to sadness and melancholy. As time passed, the phrase may have lost its reference to "Devils," which referred to depression and agitation. Blues is a genre that sounds sad, melancholy, depression, lonesome, and pity.

Rock

Originated in the United States in the 1950s, "Rock & Roll" music has become one of the most famous and influential music genres in the world. String instruments such as guitars pioneered Rock and Roll music, although other modern instruments have also contributed to its definition.

Rock and Roll music features strong and loud beats making it highly popular among the youth. Many Rock and Roll stars and star bands have gained popularity throughout the world, including Billy Haley, Little Richard, Chuck Berry, Pink Floyd, Metallica, The Doors, Megadeth, and Nirvana. Many bands have also influenced different Rock subcategories such as Punk Rock, Metal, Indie Rock, Pop Rock, and Emo.

Classical

The classical genre encompasses a variety of sub-genres. It mainly refers to orchestral styles of music between 1750 and 1820. Baroque music that prevailed rules and restrictions resulted in the emergence of classical music that somewhat differed from those rules and restrictions. Classical music is highly popular among musicians and fans due to its mesmerizing range of categories and styles.

Jazz

With origins in West African and European music identifies largely with Blues and Swing notes. It is considered one of the most original American art forms boasting a distinctive combination of interactivity and creativity. Jazz originated in the late 19th century and early 20th century, playing an important role in music when it comes to the representation of women. A range of female artists such as Betty Carter, Ella Fitzgerald, Ethel Waters, and Abbey Lincoln made the spotlight thanks to Jazz.

Country Music

Another popular genre that originated in the 1920s America is Country Music. It has its roots in Western Music and American Folk Music with the use of a range of musical instruments in use from drums and mandolin to electric guitar and mouth organ. Shania Twain, John Denver, Johnny Cash, Kenny Rogers, and Taylor Swift are some of the world's most popular country music stars.

Pop Music

Derived from the word "Popular," Pop Music is a music genre that refers to popular music. Pop music has its roots in Rock & Roll while also including a range of music forms such as country, Latin, dance to rock, and urban. Electric guitars, bass, pianos and keyboards, and synthesizer drums are largely used in Pop Music. Madonna, Michael Jackson, The Beatles, David Bowie, Elton John, Britney Spears, Beyonce, Rihanna, Justin Bieber, Lady Gaga, Taylor Swift, and Katy Perry are some of the world's most renowned Popstars.

Reggae

This genre of music originated in Jamaica in the 1960s. Bob Marley pioneered Reggae with his work and took the world by storm. Reggae music has its roots set in Jazz, RnB, and Jamaican Folk Music. Staccato Chords and offbeat rhythms largely feature in Reggae music. It also has very close links to

Afrocentric religion and Rastafarianism. In addition to Bob Marley, Peter Tosh, Gregory Isaacs, Jimmy Cliff, Bunny Wailer, and Ziggy Marley are some of the most famous Reggae musicians.

World Scales

Harmonies are melodies in music that are built using scales that are groups of musical notes that are arranged in the order of pitch or frequency. There are many different scales in the world, with the Western Music scales being the most popular and widely used in modern-day music.

Scales in Western Music are sequenced with tones and semitones with equal temperaments. As a result, there are 12 intervals in every octave, with each interval separating two tones. However, other scales in the world of music include different intervals, with most scales being based on the harmonic overtones series.

Some scales in the world consist of a different number of pitches. The Pentatonic Scale in Eastern Music only consists of five notes spanning an octave. Some scales only span a partial octave, with some of them being combined to span a full octave. Some Middle Eastern scales consist of one scales steps that span over 14 intervals, such as the Hejaz Scale. The Saba Scale consists of three consecutive steps that are separated by one semitone.

Indian music is based on a seven-note scale that is movable. Intervals are usually smaller than a semitone in Indian Rāgas. Maqamat from Arab uses quarter-tone intervals. The distance between a note and the inflection of that same note is usually less than a semitone in both Rāgas and Maqamat.

Chapter 17: Songs

Learning to play the guitar is a highly rewarding skill that revolves around practice. Therefore, guitar students must apply the chords that they learn to play songs. Many songs require a limited number of chords that are easy to play. Therefore, it should not take a long time for a guitar student to start playing songs. It can be achieved as soon as they can play and change chords fluently and correctly.

It's also that beginners keep an open mind about the songs that they learn to play on the guitar while they learn. They may not personally prefer certain genres. However, it is still important to learn easy songs and practice them as it lays the foundation for learning more difficult codes and playing more difficult songs that they like down the road.

The internet is a great resource for guitar students as they can easily find guitar tablature that is required to play songs. Many websites are dedicated to providing guitarists chord diagrams. Therefore, even if a guitar student wishes to play songs that they personally like, they can easily search the internet and find chord diagrams to play those songs.

Blues

When it comes to tradition and emotion, most other genres fail to compare to Blues. Playing Blues songs also not only enjoyable but also lays a strong foundation for many guitar skills. Here are some of the best Blues songs for beginners:

Buddy Guy -"Damn Right I've Got the Blues"

John Lee Hooker - "Boogie Chillen"

Robert Johnson - "Kindhearted Woman Blues"

Willie Dixon - "I Can't Quit You Baby"

Robert Cray - "Phone Booth"

Carl Perkins - "Matchbox"

Elmore James - "It Hurts Me Too"

Muddy Waters - "Mannish Boy"

Guitar Slim - "Things That I Used to Do"

B. B. King - "Rock Me Baby"

T Bone Walker - "T Bone Shuffle"

Eric Clapton - "Alberta"

Manish Boy - "Muddy Waters"

Robert Johnson - "Sweet Home Chicago"

B. B. King - "Sweet Little Angel"

Howlin' Wolf - "Smokestack Lightnin'"

Delmore Brothers - "Blues Stay Away from Me"

Keb Mo - "Suitcase"

Stevie Ray Vaughan - "Life by the Drop"

Howlin' Wolf - "Little Red Rooster"

Jimmy Reed - "Take Out Some Insurance"

Hank Ballard - "Look at Little Sister"

John Lee Hooker - "Boom"

Bo Didley - "Before You Accuse Me"

Rock

When it comes to music genres, Rock is one of the most loved by guitar students and music fans around the globe. It is a fairly young genre compared to some others. However, it has made a huge mark in the world of music and inspired many different sub-genres in the progress. Most guitar students are highly likely to be fans of rock music. Therefore, the following songs that are great for beginners will be very useful:

Jimmy Eat World - "The Middle"

Bob Dylan - "Knockin' On Heaven's Door"

Ritchie Valens - "La Bamba"

Tom Petty - "I Won't Back Down"

Muse - "Knights of Cydonia"

Steve Miller Band - "The Joker"

ZZ Top - "Tush"

America - "Lonely People"

The Rolling Stones -"(I Can't Get No) Satisfaction"

Creedence Clearwater Revival - "Have You Ever Seen the Rain"

The Smashing Pumpkins - "Cherub Rock"

The Animals - "House of the Rising Sun"

The Strokes - "Last Nite"

The Eagles - "Take it Easy"

The Smithereens - "Blood & Roses"

Deep Purple - "Smoke On the Water"

Buddy Holly - "Not Fade Away"

Audioslave - "Like a Stone"

Eric Clapton - "Layla"

Classical

Another great way to laying a strong foundation for a guitar student is by playing classical songs as they learn to play the guitar. They sound amazing on the guitar and can make them fall in love with the genre. Here are some of the best classical songs for beginners:

Fransisco Tárrega - "Lágrima"

Fernando Sor - "Op. 60, No. 1"

Romanza (Anonymous)

Ferdinando Carulli - "Waltz" in E Minor

Ferdinando Carulli - "Andantino" in G Major

Georg Leopold Fuhrman - "Tanz"

Ferdinando Carulli - "Andante – Opus 241"

Gaspar Sanz - "Españoleta"

Sting - "Shape of My Heart"

Ferdinando Carulli - "Country Dance"

Pink Floyd - "Is There Anybody Out There"

Bach Buree in E Minor

Peer Gynt - "In the Hall of the Mountain King"

Jazz

Many genres in music have been influenced by Jazz in some way. Therefore, learning to play some Jazz songs as beginners makes guitar players well-rounded and complete. Here are some of the best Jazz songs to play on the guitar for beginners:

Nat King Cole - "Autumn Leaves"

Duke Ellington - "Take the A Train"

Frank Sinatra - "All of Me"

Billy Holiday - "Summertime"

Sinatra & Antônio Carlos Jobim - "The Girl from Ipanema"

Nat King Cole - "There Will Never be Another You"

Billy Holiday - "Body and Soul"

Ella Fitzgerald - "Stella by Starlight"

Ella Fitzgerald - "All the Things You Are"

Frank Sinatra - "I Get a Kick Out of You"

Frank Sinatra - "Fly Me to the Moon"

Louis Armstrong - "Sweet Georgia Brown"

Ella Fitzgerald - "Have You Met Miss Jones"

Ella Fitzgerald - "Satin Doll"

Dean Martin - "Georgia on My Mind"

Ella Fitzgerald & Joe Pass - "On Green Dolphin Street"

Frank Sinatra - "They Can't Take That Away From Me"

Frank Sinatra - "Night and Day"

Dean Martin - "Bye Bye Blackbird"

Peggy Lee - "Black Coffee"

Country Music

Most guitar students are highly likely to start learning with an acoustic guitar. Country Music is a music genre that perfectly suits acoustic guitars. Here are some of the best Country songs to play on the guitar for beginners:

Carrie Underwood - "Blown Away"

Johnny Cash - "A Boy Named Sue"

Brad Paisley - "He Didn't Have to Be"

Marty Robbins - "El Paso"

Hank Williams - "Jambalaya (On the Bayou)"

Traditional - "Pay Me My Money Down"

Willie Nelson - "On the Road Again"

Tennessee Ernie Ford - "Sixteen Tons"

Steven Goodwin - "City of New Orleans"

Buck Owens - "Act Naturally"

Hank Williams - "I'm So Lonesome I Could Cry"

Willie Nelson - "Don't Fence Me In"

Merle Haggard - "The Fightin' Side of Me"

Buck Owens - "Together Again"

John Denver - "Thank God I'm a Country Boy"

Traditional - "I Shall Not Be Moved"

Pop Music

Most individuals are highly likely to appreciate Pop Music. Therefore, learning to play pop songs is a great way for guitar students to showcase their skills and find motivation. Furthermore, most guitar students are highly likely to be fans of pop music. Below are some great songs for beginners to play on the guitar:

The Beatles - "Let It Be"

Jason Mraz - "I'm Yours"

U2 - "With or Without You"

Lukas Graham - "7 Years"

Katy Perry -"Firework"

Oasis - "Wonderwall"

MGMT - "Kids"

Twenty-One Pilots - "Ride"

John Legend - "All of Me"

Taylor Swift - "You Need To Calm Down"

Wilson Pickett - "Land of a Thousand Dances"

The National - "I Need My Girl"

Andra Day - "Rise Up"

Camila Cabello - "Havana"

Thompson Twins - "Hold Me Now"

Ben Kweller - "Thirteen"

Taylor Swift - "Wildest Dreams"

Maren Morris - "My Church"

Jamie Lawson - "I Wasn't Expecting That"

The Zombies - "Time of the Season"

Van Morrison - "Brown Eyed Girl"

Anna Kendrick - "When I'm Gone"

Fleetwood Mac - "Don't Stop"

Buffalo Springfield - "For What It's Worth"

Bruno Mars - "The Lazy Song"

Ed Sheeran - "Give Me Love"

Justin Bieber - "Love Yourself"

George Ezra - "Listen To the Man"

Conclusion

Reaching the conclusion of this book suggests that the reader is highly likely to have already mastered all the essential skills that are required to reach the intermediate level after starting out as a beginner. Therefore, it is highly likely to be apparent that this book kept its promise of helping guitar students learn how to play the guitar with clear instructions and tips while ensuring that they receive a well-rounded knowledge about the guitar and music in general.

The importance of making a real commitment to learning to play the guitar was highlighted at the very beginning of this book. It's impossible to master the guitar without making a real commitment even for the naturally gifted beginners. Many other factors, such as discipline, knowledge, patience, and persistence, were similarly highlighted, and they may have contributed to the reader's success in learning to play the guitar.

Purchasing a guitar is one of the most important early steps that beginners take to learn to play the guitar. Borrowing someone else's guitar usually indicates a lack of commitment and confidence. Therefore, it should be avoided unless a guitar student does not have the budget to purchase a good guitar. It must also be reminded that cheap guitars do more bad than good for beginners. Therefore, the reader may now understand how the money invested in buying a good guitar and the essential accessories contributed to their success.

Reaching the intermediate level may require guitar students to consider going for an upgrade depending on the quality of the guitar that they purchased as a beginner. Most of the instructions and tips for those who are looking to buy a guitar can be followed when purchasing the second guitar.

Furthermore, the reader is highly likely to make a better choice the second time around since they understand more about guitars and understand more about the "feel" of a guitar.

Music Theory is a topic that most guitar students and even some guitar coaches prefer to skip. Music theory can indeed be somewhat boring for most students. However, it's difficult and ineffective to try to learn the guitar without a good understanding of music theory. As a result, the lesson was covered at the very beginning of the book, while explaining the theory in the simplest and most fun way possible for the reader.

Learning to play the guitar requires guitar students to have a good understanding of guitars out there without being limited to their own guitars. The reader was taken through different types of guitars and the type of sound they create so that they understand, which guitars to add to their collection down the road.

Another highly important lesson regarding tuning the guitar was covered early in the guide to ensure that students do not practice with guitars that are out of tune. Different tuning methods from very basic to intermediate were discussed using simple steps. It's highly advised that guitar students learn a combination of tuning methods, especially given the fact that they have now reached the intermediate level.

Power chords are some of the coolest sounding guitar chords. A chapter was dedicated to this book to educate the reader about power chords, their history, famous uses, terminology, techniques, and fingering. Mastering power chords was also identified as a stepping stone to learning and playing barre chords that most guitar students find highly challenging. The reader was provided with a well-rounded lesson on Barre Chords, just like Power Chords, to ensure that they are able to learn them assisted by correct technique and tricks as well as the magic ingredients, patience, and persistence.

Open chords sound fuller and unique when played. Furthermore, a large number of songs can be played with open chords, although a few other types of chords may exist here and there. The reader was provided with a complete overview of the Major Scale and Minor Scale open chords to ensure that they are able to play songs using open chords freely.

There are many other types of guitar chords in addition to Power Chords, Major Chords, Minor Chords, and Barre Chords that guitar students must learn to be able to play different songs and progress to the intermediate level. These types of chords were comprehensively discussed in the book paving the way for students to learn and apply those chords.

Some guitar students put a lot of emphasis on learning chords when learning to play the guitar that they neglect training their strumming hands. Correct strumming is an integral part of becoming a good guitarist. Different right-hand strumming techniques were discussed in-depth with many tips to ensure that the reader is able to master different strumming techniques.

Although it is possible to strum with fingertips, plectrums are important as they help guitarists create louder and clearer sounds when playing the guitar. Playing notes is also made easy when using picks. The book discusses plectrums in detail while providing the reader with a wealth of knowledge regarding plectrums, including different types of plectrums and how they affect the sound that the guitar creates and how to hold a pick correctly.

Developing a correct left-hand technique is another very important lesson for beginners as it enables them to play notes and chords freely, comfortably, and smoothly. The correct left-hand technique was discussed in the book while providing the reader with a number of valuable tips to ensure that their left-hand technique is correct.

Many beginners put a lot of focus on learning chords as it enables them to play their favorite songs. However, learning to play the guitar includes smoothly playing different notes that open doors to guitar students developing to become lead guitarists as they reach the intermediate level. Furthermore, playing notes and note patterns improve the movement of fingers on the fingerboard that significantly contributes to the overall progress of guitar students.

Different single-note patterns and scales are discussed in the book to ensure that guitar students develop a great understanding of notes and patterns on the guitar. Practicing scales and note patterns make creates well-rounded guitarists and open them the option of progressing to play lead guitar.

The character of the sound is a big part of the music. Articulations enable musicians to add character to the sound they create. Articulations are discussed in length so that guitar students can become better guitarists while comfortably applying different techniques related to articulations in their playing.

Similarly, improvisation is a skill that most guitar guides and lessons skip since it requires certain levels of skill and knowledge and involves hard work. A chapter is dedicated to improvisation to ensure that the reader starts improvising with the guitar that leads to the birth of a more complete guitarist.

As guitar students grow, they are highly encouraged to improvise to reach higher levels of guitar playing.

Most guitar students likely have a limited understanding of different music genres. They may prefer certain genres over others and prefer to play songs belonging to certain genres and avoid others. However, it is highly recommended that guitar students are open-minded regarding genres when learning to play the guitar. Listening to different genres and learning to play songs belonging to various genres makes them more versatile guitarists with defined taste in music.

Guitar students often don't know the types of songs that are more suitable for beginners. The book provides a list of over 100 songs that are perfect for beginners while making sure that songs from the most popular genres are included so that the reader can practice using songs belonging to different genres.

This guide to learning the guitar is focused on providing guitar students the knowledge that they required to master the art of playing the guitar. The lessons are structured in such a way that guitar students are able to apply the knowledge they gain and practice before progressing to the lessons that follow. Therefore, it is highly recommended that guitar students practice and develop different skills as they progress reading the book. If a reader goes through this guide in one go without application, it is highly recommended that they re-read the guide while focusing on application to be more successful.

Being able to play the guitar has many benefits. It's one of the most satisfying skills that a man or woman can develop. It is a highly rewarding activity as a lot of hard work and time goes into it. Becoming a guitarist requires a lot of hard work, time, patience, and persistence. Therefore, it is important to remind the reader to continue with their work ethic on to the intermediate level so that they continue to grow to become a great guitarist one day.

Discover "How to Find Your Sound"

http://musicprod.ontrapages.com/

Swindali music coaching/Skype lessons.

Email djswindali@gmail.com for info and pricing

www.ingramcontent.com/pod-product-compliance
Lightning Source LLC
LaVergne TN
LVHW021100090525
810839LV00008B/522